M000122173

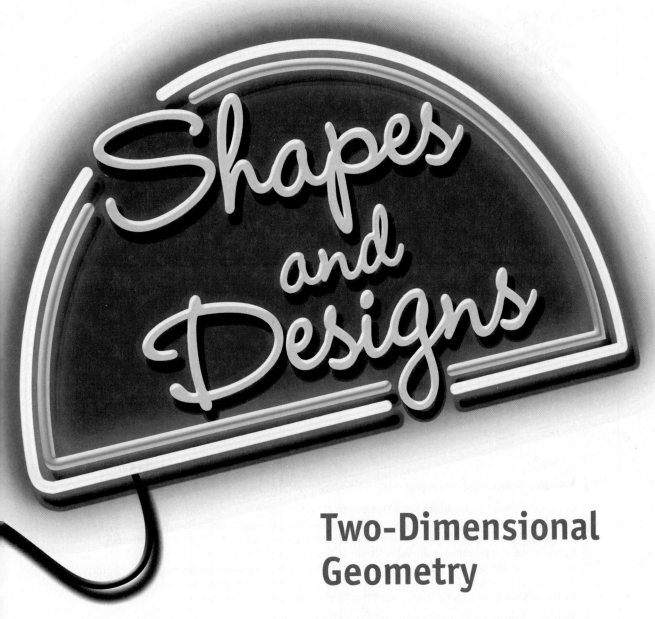

Two-Dimensional Geometry

Glenda Lappan, Elizabeth Difanis Phillips,
James T. Fey, Susan N. Friel

Pearson

Boston, Massachusetts

Connected Mathematics® was developed at Michigan State University with financial support from the Michigan State University Office of the Provost, Computing and Technology, and the College of Natural Science.

This material is based upon work supported by the National Science Foundation under Grant No. MDR 9150217 and Grant No. ESI 9986372. Opinions expressed are those of the authors and not necessarily those of the Foundation.

As with prior editions of this work, the authors and administration of Michigan State University preserve a tradition of devoting royalties from this publication to support activities sponsored by the MSU Mathematics Education Enrichment Fund.

Acknowledgments appear on page 107, which constitutes an extension of this copyright page.

13-digit ISBN 978-0-328-90045-9
10-digit ISBN 0-328-90045-1

2 17

Authors

A Team of Experts

....

Glenda Lappan is a University Distinguished Professor in the Program in Mathematics Education (PRIME) and the Department of Mathematics at Michigan State University. Her research and development interests are in the connected areas of students' learning of mathematics and mathematics teachers' professional growth and change related to the development and enactment of K–12 curriculum materials.

Elizabeth Difanis Phillips is a Senior Academic Specialist in the Program in Mathematics Education (PRIME) and the Department of Mathematics at Michigan State University. She is interested in teaching and learning mathematics for both teachers and students. These interests have led to curriculum and professional development projects at the middle school and high school levels, as well as projects related to the teaching and learning of algebra across the grades.

James T. Fey is a Professor Emeritus at the University of Maryland. His consistent professional interest has been development and research focused on curriculum materials that engage middle and high school students in problem-based collaborative investigations of mathematical ideas and their applications.

Susan N. Friel is a Professor of Mathematics Education in the School of Education at the University of North Carolina at Chapel Hill. Her research interests focus on statistics education for middle-grade students and, more broadly, on teachers' professional development and growth in teaching mathematics K–8.

With... Yvonne Grant and Jacqueline Stewart

Yvonne Grant teaches mathematics at Portland Middle School in Portland, Michigan. Jacqueline Stewart is a recently retired high school teacher of mathematics at Okemos High School in Okemos, Michigan. Both Yvonne and Jacqueline have worked on a variety of activities related to the development, implementation, and professional development of the CMP curriculum since its beginning in 1991.

Development Team

CMP3 Authors

Glenda Lappan, University Distinguished Professor, Michigan State University
Elizabeth Difanis Phillips, Senior Academic Specialist, Michigan State University
James T. Fey, Professor Emeritus, University of Maryland
Susan N. Friel, Professor, University of North Carolina – Chapel Hill

With...
Yvonne Grant, Portland Middle School, Michigan
Jacqueline Stewart, Mathematics Consultant, Mason, Michigan

In Memory of... William M. Fitzgerald, Professor (Deceased), Michigan State University, who made substantial contributions to conceptualizing and creating CMP1.

Administrative Assistant

Michigan State University
Judith Martus Miller

Support Staff

Michigan State University
Undergraduate Assistants:
Bradley Robert Corlett, Carly Fleming,
Erin Lucian, Scooter Nowak

Development Assistants

Michigan State University
Graduate Research Assistants:
Richard "Abe" Edwards, Nic Gilbertson,
Funda Gonulates, Aladar Horvath,
Eun Mi Kim, Kevin Lawrence, Jennifer
Nimtz, Joanne Philhower, Sasha Wang

Assessment Team

Maine
Falmouth Public Schools
Falmouth Middle School: Shawn Towle

Michigan
Ann Arbor Public Schools
Tappan Middle School
Anne Marie Nicoll-Turner

Portland Public Schools
Portland Middle School
Holly DeRosia, Yvonne Grant

Traverse City Area Public Schools
Traverse City East Middle School
Jane Porath, Mary Beth Schmitt

Traverse City West Middle School
Jennifer Rundio, Karrie Tufts

Ohio
Clark-Shawnee Local Schools
Rockway Middle School: Jim Mamer

Content Consultants

Michigan State University
Peter Lappan, Professor Emeritus,
Department of Mathematics

Normandale Community College
Christopher Danielson, Instructor,
Department of Mathematics & Statistics

University of North Carolina – Wilmington
Dargan Frierson, Jr., Professor, Department
of Mathematics & Statistics

Student Activities
Michigan State University
Brin Keller, Associate Professor,
Department of Mathematics

Consultants

Indiana
Purdue University
Mary Bouck, Mathematics Consultant

Michigan
Oakland Schools
Valerie Mills, Mathematics Education
Supervisor
Mathematics Education Consultants:
Geraldine Devine, Dana Gosen

Ellen Bacon, Independent Mathematics
Consultant

New York
University of Rochester
Jeffrey Choppin, Associate Professor

Ohio
University of Toledo
Debra Johanning, Associate Professor

Pennsylvania
University of Pittsburgh
Margaret Smith, Professor

Texas
University of Texas at Austin
Emma Trevino, Supervisor of
Mathematics Programs, The Dana Center

Mathematics for All Consulting
Carmen Whitman, Mathematics Consultant

Reviewers

Michigan
Ionia Public Schools
Kathy Dole, Director of Curriculum
and Instruction

Grand Valley State University
Lisa Kasmer, Assistant Professor

Portland Public Schools
Teri Keusch, Classroom Teacher

Minnesota
Hopkins School District 270
Michele Luke, Mathematics Coordinator

Field Test Sites for CMP3

Michigan
Ann Arbor Public Schools
Tappan Middle School
Anne Marie Nicoll-Turner*

Portland Public Schools
Portland Middle School: Mark Braun,
Angela Buckland, Holly DeRosia,
Holly Feldpausch, Angela Foote,
Yvonne Grant*, Kristin Roberts,
Angie Stump, Tammi Wardwell

Traverse City Area Public Schools
Traverse City East Middle School
Ivanka Baic Berkshire, Brenda Dunscombe,
Tracie Herzberg, Deb Larimer, Jan Palkowski,
Rebecca Perreault, Jane Porath*,
Robert Sagan, Mary Beth Schmitt*

Traverse City West Middle School
Pamela Alfieri, Jennifer Rundio,
Maria Taplin, Karrie Tufts*

Maine
Falmouth Public Schools
Falmouth Middle School: Sally Bennett,
Chris Driscoll, Sara Jones, Shawn Towle*

Minnesota
Minneapolis Public Schools
Jefferson Community School
Leif Carlson*,
Katrina Hayek Munsisoumang*

Ohio
Clark-Shawnee Local Schools
Reid School: Joanne Gilley
Rockway Middle School: Jim Mamer*
Possum School: Tami Thomas

*Indicates a Field Test Site Coordinator

Two-Dimensional Geometry

Looking Ahead 2

Mathematical Highlights 4

Mathematical Practices and Habits of Mind 5

Unit Project: What I Know About Shapes and Designs 7

1 The Family of Polygons   8

1.1 Sorting and Sketching Polygons 9

1.2 In a Spin Angles and Rotations 10

1.3 Estimating Measures of Rotations and Angles 16

1.4 Measuring Angles 19

1.5 Design Challenge I Drawing With Tools—Ruler and Protractor........... 23

Ⓐ Ⓒ Ⓔ Homework 24

Mathematical Reflections 39

2 Designing Polygons: The Angle Connection   41

2.1 Angle Sums of Regular Polygons............................. 41

2.2 Angle Sums of Any Polygon 45

2.3 The Bees Do It Polygons in Nature........................ 47

2.4 The Ins and Outs of Polygons................................ 49

Ⓐ Ⓒ Ⓔ Homework 52

Mathematical Reflections 60

Designing Triangles and Quadrilaterals 62

3.1 Building Triangles...63

3.2 Design Challenge II Drawing Triangles..................................64

3.3 Building Quadrilaterals..66

3.4 Parallel Lines and Transversals...69

3.5 Design Challenge III The Quadrilateral Game..................72

Ⓐ Ⓒ Ⓔ Homework 76

Mathematical Reflections 87

Looking Back 89

English/Spanish Glossary 92

Index 104

Acknowledgments 107

Looking Ahead

How can mathematics be used to measure the difficulty of spins and flips by snow boarders and skate boarders?

What properties of a regular hexagon make it the shape of choice for the cells of a honeycomb?

Why are braces on towers, roofs, and bridges in the shapes of triangles and not rectangles or pentagons?

Objects in nature and designs are outlined and covered by an endless variety of geometric shapes. But some shapes have properties that make them especially important in science, engineering, construction, crafts, and arts. In your work on the Investigations of this Unit you will discover the special importance of *polygons*. Polygons are planar geometric shapes formed by linking points called *vertices* with line segments called *sides*.

Many of the Problems will focus on triangles and quadrilaterals. You will build models and use rulers and protractors to draw shapes meeting given conditions. These construction and drawing experiments will show why triangles are frequently used in engineering and construction.

You will also examine patterns in the measures of interior and exterior angles in regular and irregular polygons. You will develop formulas to find those angle measures without actually measuring. While working with interior and exterior angles of polygons, you will use facts about supplementary, adjacent, and vertical angles to find angle measures.

Mathematical Highlights

Shapes and Designs

The Problems of this Unit explore properties of polygons. Through work on tasks that require drawing, building, measuring, and reasoning about the size and shape of polygons, you will learn:

- How to sort polygons into classes according to the number, size, and relationships of their sides and angles

- How to find angle measures by estimation, by use of tools like protractors and angle rulers, and by reasoning with variables and equations

- Formulas for finding the sum of the interior and exterior angles in any polygon

- The relationships of complementary and supplementary pairs of angles, such as those formed by interior and exterior angles of polygons, and in figures where parallel lines are cut by transversals

- How to apply and design angle-side measurement conditions needed for drawing triangles and quadrilaterals with specific properties

- The symmetry, tiling, and rigidity or flexibility properties of polygons that make them useful in buildings, tools, art and craft designs, and natural objects

As you work on the Problems in this Unit, ask yourself these questions about situations that involve shapes.

What do these polygons have in common? **How** do they differ from each other?

When should I use estimation, freehand drawing, or special tools to measure and construct angles and polygons?

How do the side lengths and angles of polygons determine their shapes?

Why do certain polygons appear so often in buildings, artistic designs, and natural objects?

How can I give directions for constructing polygons that meet conditions of any given problem?

Mathematical Practices and Habits of Mind

In the *Connected Mathematics* curriculum you will develop an understanding of important mathematical ideas by solving problems and reflecting on the mathematics involved. Every day, you will use "habits of mind" to make sense of problems and apply what you learn to new situations. Some of these habits are described by the *Common Core State Standards for Mathematical Practices* (MP).

MP1 Make sense of problems and persevere in solving them.

When using mathematics to solve a problem, it helps to think carefully about

- data and other facts you are given and what additional information you need to solve the problem;
- strategies you have used to solve similar problems and whether you could solve a related simpler problem first;
- how you could express the problem with equations, diagrams, or graphs;
- whether your answer makes sense.

MP2 Reason abstractly and quantitatively.

When you are asked to solve a problem, it often helps to

- focus first on the key mathematical ideas;
- check that your answer makes sense in the problem setting;
- use what you know about the problem setting to guide your mathematical reasoning.

MP3 Construct viable arguments and critique the reasoning of others.

When you are asked to explain why a conjecture is correct, you can

- show some examples that fit the claim and explain why they fit;
- show how a new result follows logically from known facts and principles.

When you believe a mathematical claim is incorrect, you can

- show one or more counterexamples—cases that don't fit the claim;
- find steps in the argument that do not follow logically from prior claims.

MP4 Model with mathematics.

When you are asked to solve problems, it often helps to

- think carefully about the numbers or geometric shapes that are the most important factors in the problem, then ask yourself how those factors are related to each other;
- express data and relationships in the problem with tables, graphs, diagrams, or equations, and check your result to see if it makes sense.

MP5 Use appropriate tools strategically.

When working on mathematical questions, you should always

- decide which tools are most helpful for solving the problem and why;
- try a different tool when you get stuck.

MP6 Attend to precision.

In every mathematical exploration or problem-solving task, it is important to

- think carefully about the required accuracy of results; is a number estimate or geometric sketch good enough, or is a precise value or drawing needed?
- report your discoveries with clear and correct mathematical language that can be understood by those to whom you are speaking or writing.

MP7 Look for and make use of structure.

In mathematical explorations and problem solving, it is often helpful to

- look for patterns that show how data points, numbers, or geometric shapes are related to each other;
- use patterns to make predictions.

MP8 Look for and express regularity in repeated reasoning.

When results of a repeated calculation show a pattern, it helps to

- express that pattern as a general rule that can be used in similar cases;
- look for shortcuts that will make the calculation simpler in other cases.

You will use all of the Mathematical Practices in this Unit. Sometimes, when you look at a Problem, it is obvious which practice is most helpful. At other times, you will decide on a practice to use during class explorations and discussions. After completing each Problem, ask yourself:

- What mathematics have I learned by solving this Problem?
- What Mathematical Practices were helpful in learning this mathematics?

Unit Project

What I Know About Shapes and Designs

As you work in this Unit, you will be asked to think about the characteristics of different shapes. You will determine how unusual a shape can be and still be a triangle, quadrilateral, pentagon, or hexagon. You will also be asked to think about the relationships among these shapes. It is these characteristics of shapes and the relationships among them that affect the designs you see in your world.

One of the ways you will be asked to demonstrate your understanding of the mathematics in the Unit is through a final project. At the end of the Unit, you will use what you have learned to create a project. Your project can be a story, a book, a poster, a report, a mobile, a movie, or a slide show.

The Family of Polygons

This Unit is about the properties and uses of geometric figures called *polygons*. Some shapes below are polygons and some are not.

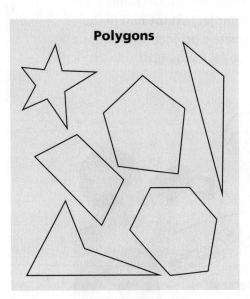

Polygons

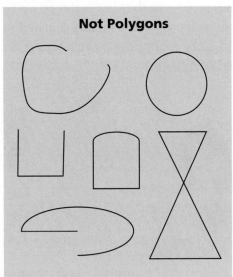

Not Polygons

- How do you describe differences between polygons and non-polygons?

- What test would you use to decide if a figure is or is not a polygon?

- What familiar objects have shapes like the polygon examples?

- What other shapes are examples of polygons and non-polygons?

....

Common Core State Standards

7.G.A.2 Draw (freehand, with ruler and protractor, and with technology) geometric shapes with given conditions . . .

1.1 Sorting and Sketching Polygons

Polygons come in many shapes and sizes. The set of 22 shapes shown here is only a sample of the infinite variety of polygons. Polygons are used in practical, artistic, and scientific shapes and designs.

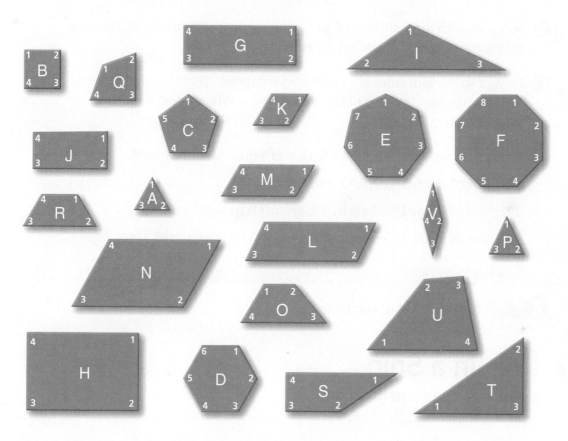

Mathematicians classify and name groups of polygons with similar properties.

Problem 1.1

Ⓐ Sort the polygons in the Shapes Set into groups that have one or more properties in common.

   1. Describe the properties shared by the members of each group.

   2. Sketch another shape that belongs in each group.

Ⓑ Polygons with three sides (and three angles) are called *triangles*. How are the triangles in the Shapes Set different from each other?

Ⓒ Polygons with four sides are called *quadrilaterals*. Sort the quadrilaterals in the Shapes Set into two or more subgroups. What properties do the subgroup members share?

Ⓓ A group of students put shapes R, O, and S into the same group.

   1. What properties do R, O, and S share?

   2. Would shape Q belong in this group? Why or why not?

   3. Would shape L belong in this group? Why or why not?

ⒶⒸⒺ Homework starts on page 24.

1.2 In a Spin
Angles and Rotations

The shape of any polygon depends on the number and length of its sides. The shape also depends on the angles at which those sides meet. Here are two quadrilaterals with identical side lengths, but different shapes.

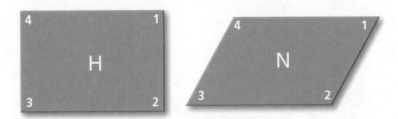

The term *polygon* is a Greek word that means "many angles." You will look at how the side lengths and angles affect the shape of a polygon. To begin, you will explore angles.

The *X-Games* are popular summer and winter sports events. Contestants perform spectacular jumps, flips, and spins on skateboards, snowboards, motorcycles, bicycles, and even snowmobiles. Judges, competitors, and fans describe the challenge of a flip or spin with numbers like 180, 360, 540, 720, 900, or 1080.

Snowboard Rotation

Measuring flips and spins involves thinking about an angle as a change in direction called a *rotation*. In mathematics, you measure an angle or a rotation with a unit called the **degree.** Rotation angles are measured from 0 degrees to 360 degrees or more to indicate turns from a small amount to one full turn (and more).

You measure rotation angles in a counterclockwise direction. A rotation angle has an *initial* and a *terminal side*. The initial side is the ray showing the starting direction while the terminal side is the ray showing the ending direction after the rotation.

A one-quarter rotation is 90°. A **right angle** measures 90°. Right angles are commonly marked with a small square. Suppose you draw a ray to divide a right angle into two angles of equal measure. Each angle would be a 45° acute angle.

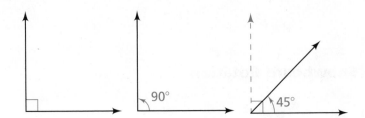

Suppose you draw 89 rays to divide a right angle into 90 angles of equal measure. Each angle would have a measure of 1°.

A rotation of one-half turn defines a *straight angle*. It measures 180°.

Recall that angles whose measures are less than 90° are called *acute angles*. Angles whose measures are between 90° and 180° are called *obtuse angles*.

- Can you jump and turn through angles of 90°, 180°, 270°, or even 360°?

Did You Know?

The ancient Babylonians measured angles in degrees. They set the measure of an angle that goes all the way around a point to 360°. They may have chosen 360° because their number system was based on the number 60. They may have also considered the fact that the number 360 has many factors. This makes it easy to measure many fractions of full turns.

Estimating and measuring rotation angles is easier if you know some *benchmark angles*. Playing the Four in a Row game will help you build your angle sense. The Four in a Row game is played on the circular grids shown below.

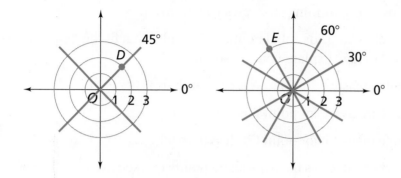

The grid on the left has lines at 45° intervals. The grid on the right has lines at 30° intervals. The circles are numbered 1, 2, and 3 as you move out from the center at 0. Point *D* has coordinates (2, 45°).

• What are the coordinates for the location of point *E*?

Four in a Row

Directions

Choose one of the circular grids. The grids have either 30° or 45° intervals.

• Player A chooses a point where a circle and grid line meet. Then Player A says the coordinates of the point.

• Player B checks that the coordinates Player A gave are correct. If they are, Player A marks the point with an X. If they are not, Player A does not mark the point.

• Player B chooses a point and says its coordinates. If the coordinates are correct, Player B marks the point with an O.

• Players continue to take turns, saying the coordinates of points and marking the points.

• The first player to get four marks in a row, either along a grid line or around a circle, wins the game.

Problem 1.2

A Play Four in a Row several times. Play games with the 30° grid and the 45° grid. Write down any winning strategies you discover.

On one of the circular grids, label points A, B, and C that fit the descriptions in parts (1)–(3) below. Explain your reasoning.

1. The angle measure for point A is greater than 120°.

2. The angle measure for point B is equal to 0°.

3. The angle measure for point C is less than 90°.

4. Will everyone in class have the same points marked? Why or why not?

B In the Four in a Row game, the circular grids have horizontal and vertical axes. They divide the playing area into four sectors called *quadrants*.

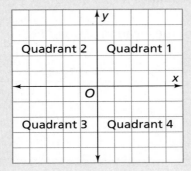

What can you say about measures of rotation angles with the first side on the positive *x*-axis (to the right) and second side in each quadrant below?

1. Quadrant 1

2. Quadrant 2

3. Quadrant 3

4. Quadrant 4

ACE Homework starts on page 24.

Did You Know?

The circular grids used to play Four in a Row are examples of polar coordinate systems. Sir Isaac Newton used polar coordinates in his contributions to mathematics and science.

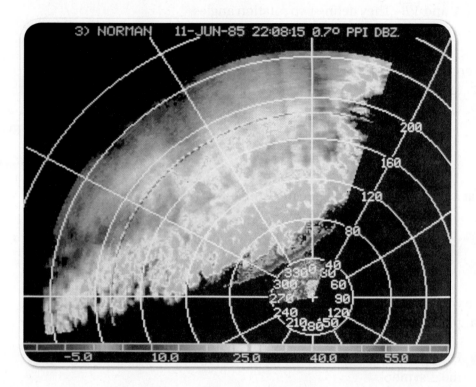

Polar coordinates are commonly used to locate ships at sea, planes in the air, or rain and snowstorms. An object appearing on a radar screen is a moving point or region. It has direction (in degrees) and distance from the radar site.

1.3 Estimating Measures of Rotations and Angles

The next sketch shows two rays with a common endpoint. The rays are named $\overrightarrow{VA}$ and $\overrightarrow{VB}$. They define two rotation angles.

The angle named $\angle AVB$ is a counterclockwise turn from ray $\overrightarrow{VA}$ to ray $\overrightarrow{VB}$.

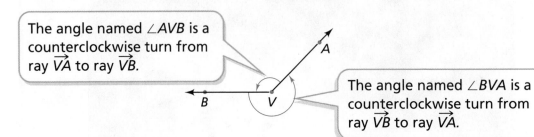

The angle named $\angle BVA$ is a counterclockwise turn from ray $\overrightarrow{VB}$ to ray $\overrightarrow{VA}$.

- What is the approximate degree measure of $\angle AVB$? Of $\angle BVA$?

Problem 1.3

Use what you know about measurement and naming of rotation angles to complete the Problem.

A Estimate the measure of each angle in degrees. Name each angle with the $\angle$ symbol.

1.

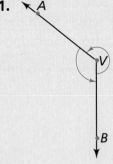

2.

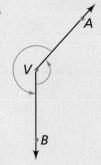

3.

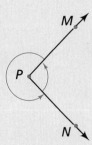

4.

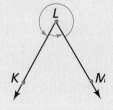

Problem 1.3 *continued*

B Sketch a rotation angle with approximately the given measure.

1. 220°
2. 270°
3. 150°
4. 300°

C Sketch each angle described. Find its measure in degrees.

1. one third of a right angle
2. one and a half times a right angle
3. three times a right angle
4. three and a half times a right angle
5. two thirds of a straight angle
6. one and two thirds times a right angle
7. one and a sixth times a straight angle
8. twice a straight angle

D For each rotation described, find its measure in degrees.

1. 1.5 turns
2. 2 turns
3. 1.25 turns

A C E Homework starts on page 24.

Did You Know?

Honeybees live in colonies. Each colony has a single queen and thousands of worker bees. The worker bees find flowers to get nectar. The nectar is used to make honey. Worker bees build the honeycomb and keep the beehive clean. They feed and groom the queen bee and take care of the young. They also guard the hive against intruders.

Scientific observation has shown that honeybees give each other directions to flowers by performing a lively dance!

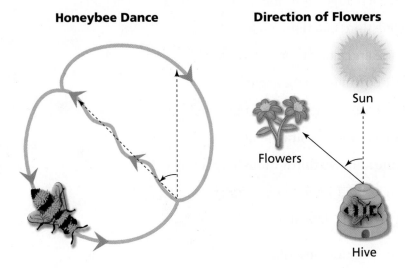

Honeybee Dance

Direction of Flowers

Sun

Flowers

Hive

The messenger bee in the center shows the other bees the direction and distance from the hive to nectar. The bee does a dance called the figure-eight waggle. Worker bees watching the dance learn where to find nectar to make honey.

The dancing bee communicates the direction and distance to fly from the hive. The bee makes two semi-circles. He waggles along the straight run, the path through the center of his dance.

The angle in the dance made between the straight run and the direction of gravity is the direction. This is because the beehive is oriented vertically, not horizontally. The length of the straight run is proportional to the distance.

1.4 Measuring Angles

One common tool to use for measuring angles is the *angle ruler*. An angle ruler has two arms linked by a rivet. The rivet allows the arms to spread apart to form angles of various sizes. One arm is marked with a circular ruler showing degree measures from 0° to 360°.

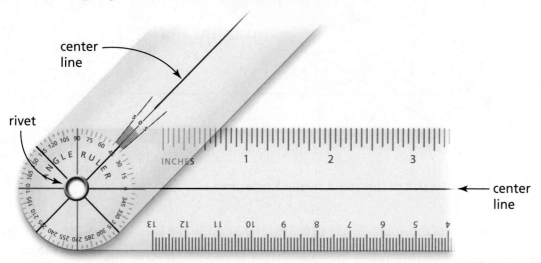

To measure an angle with an angle ruler:

- First place the rivet over the vertex.

- Set the *center line* of the arm marked as a ruler on the first side of the angle.

- Swing the other arm counterclockwise until its center line lies on the second side of the angle.

- Read the angle measure on the circular ruler.

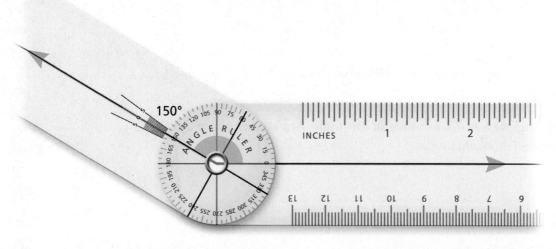

When you use an angle ruler to measure a polygon in the Shapes Set or another object, place the object between the two arms of the angle ruler.

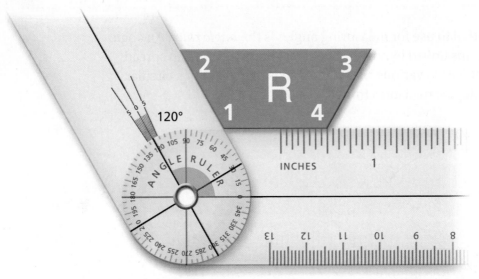

Read the size of the angle, Angle 1 measures 120° in shape R.

Then, read the size of the angle. Angle 1 measures 120° in shape R.

Another tool for measuring angles in degrees is the *protractor*. It is usually semi-circular and has a scale in degrees. The protractor below shows how to measure ∠AVB.

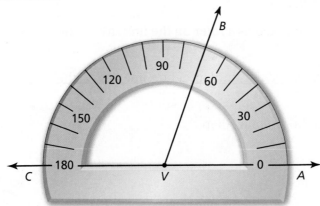

- What is the measure of ∠AVB in degrees?

Notice in the diagram above that ∠CVB and ∠AVB share a side. Both angles have $\overrightarrow{VB}$ as a side of the angle. Angles that share a side are called *adjacent angles*.

Problem 1.4

A For each polygon shape shown below, *estimate* the measure of each angle. Sketch each figure and label the angles with your estimates.

B 1. Use an angle ruler to *measure* each of the angles from Question A.

2. Compare your estimates from Question A with your measurements. If your estimate and measurement differ by more than 10°, measure that angle again and check your work.

C Find measures of the angles shown in the diagram.

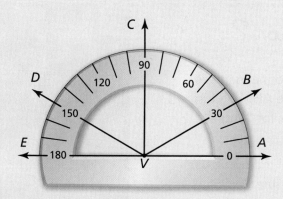

1. ∠AVB
2. ∠AVC
3. ∠AVD
4. ∠BVC
5. ∠BVD
6. ∠CVD

D If the measures of two angles add to 90°, they are called **complementary angles.** If the measures of two angles add to 180°, they are called **supplementary angles.**

1. Name the pairs of complementary angles in the diagram of Question C.

2. Name the pairs of supplementary angles in the diagram of Question C.

continued on the next page >

Problem **1.4** continued

E Find the measures of the angles. Use an angle ruler or a protractor.

1.

2.

3.

4.

A C E Homework starts on page 24.

Did You Know?

The angle ruler's formal name is *goniometer* (goh nee AHM uh tur). Goniometer is Greek for "angle measurer."

Doctors and physical therapists use goniometers to measure flexibility (range of motion) in knees, elbows, fingers, and other joints.

1.5 Design Challenge I
Drawing with Tools—Ruler and Protractor

Some problems challenge you to use tools to draw figures that are only described in words. For those problems, you can use line and angle rulers or protractors to accurately draw side lengths and angle measures.

Problem 1.5

A Draw an angle for each measure.

  1. 25°

  2. 175°

  3. 200°

  4. On the drawing for part (1), show a complement and a supplement of the angle.

B The symbol △ABC names a triangle with vertices A, B, and C. Draw each of the polygons, if possible.

  1. △ABC with $\overline{AB}$ = 1 in., $\overline{BC}$ = 1.5 in., and ∠CBA = 35°

  2. a rectangle with base 2 in. and height 1 in.

  3. a triangle with angles 45° and 60° and one side of length 2 in.

  4. a parallelogram with two sides of length 2 in., two sides of length 1 in., and angles of 60° and 120°

  5. △KLM with side KL = 1 in., side LM = 1.5 in., ∠KLM = 135°, and side KM = 1 in.

  6. a triangle with all sides of length 1.5 in. and all angles of 60°

C For each part below, and any polygon you choose, write one set of directions that are:

  1. satisfied by only one unique shape.

  2. satisfied by two or more different shapes.

  3. not satisfied by any shape.

A C E Homework starts on page 24.

Applications

1. Tell whether each figure is a polygon. Explain how you know.

a.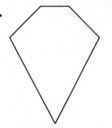

b.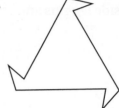

c.

d.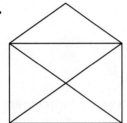

e.

f.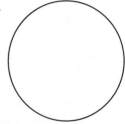

2. Copy and complete the table. Sort the Shapes Set into groups by polygon name.

Common Polygons

Number of Sides	Polygon Name	Examples in the Shapes Set
3	triangle	■
4	quadrilateral	■
5	pentagon	■
6	hexagon	■
7	heptagon	■
8	octagon	■
9	nonagon	■
10	decagon	■
12	dodecagon	■

3. A figure is called a *regular polygon* if all sides are the same length and all angles are equal. List the members of the Shapes Set that are regular polygons.

4. Name the polygons used in these street and highway signs (ignore slightly rounded corners).

a.

b.

c.

d.

e.

f.

g.

h.

i.

5. An angle whose measure is less than 90° is called an *acute angle*. An angle whose measure is greater than 90° and less than 180° is called an *obtuse angle*. Which of these angles are acute, which are obtuse, and which are right?

a.

b.
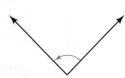

c.

d.
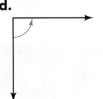

e.

f.

6. For two different angles, the angle with the greater turn from one side to the other is considered the larger angle. A test question asked to choose the larger angle.

Angle 1 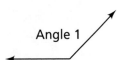   Angle 2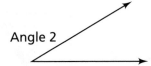

In one class, most students chose Angle 2. Do you agree? Why or why not?

7. List all polygons in the Shapes Set that have:

   a. only right angle corners.

   b. only obtuse angle corners.

   c. only acute angle corners.

   d. at least one angle of each type—acute, right, and obtuse.

8. Snowboarders use angle measures to describe their flips and spins. Explain what a snowboarder would mean by each statement.

   a. I did a 720.   **b.** I did a 540.   **c.** I did a 180.

9. Which benchmark angles (multiples of 30° or 45°) are closest to the rotation angles below?

   a. 40°   **b.** 140°   **c.** 175°

   d. 220°   **e.** 250°   **f.** 310°

10. In parts (a)–(h), decide whether each angle is closest to 30°, 60°, 90°, 120°, 150°, 180°, 270°, or 360° without measuring. Explain your reasoning.

   a.    **b.**

   c.    **d.**

   e. 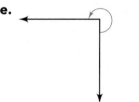   **f.**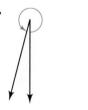

   g. 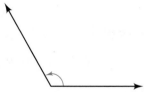   **h.**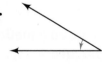

   i. For each angle in parts (a)–(h), classify them as right, acute, or obtuse.

11. Give the degree measure of each angle.

    a. one sixth of a right angle   **b.** three fourths of a right angle

    c. five fourths of a right angle   **d.** five thirds of a right angle

    e. two thirds of a full turn   **f.** one and a half full turns

12. For each pair of angles in parts (a)–(d), estimate the measure of each angle. Then, check your estimates by measuring with an angle ruler or a protractor.

a.
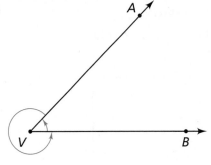

b.
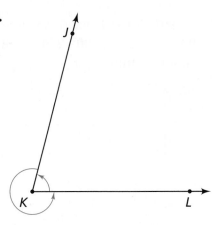

c.

d.
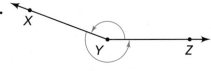

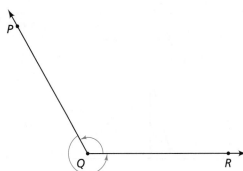

For Exercises 13–16, write an equation and find the measure of the angle labeled *x*, *without* measuring.

13.
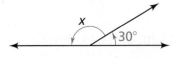

14.
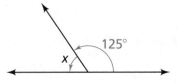

15.
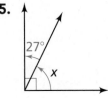

16.

17. At the start of each hour, the minute hand points straight up at 12. In parts (a)–(f), determine the angle between the minute hand at the start of an hour and the minute hand after the given amount of time passes. For each situation, sketch the angle and indicate the rotation of the minute hand.

- **a.** 15 minutes
- **b.** 30 minutes
- **c.** 20 minutes
- **d.** one hour
- **e.** 5 minutes
- **f.** one and one-half hours

18. One common definition of an angle is two rays with a common endpoint. There are many times when you are really interested in the region or area between the two rays. For example, when a pizza is cut into six or eight pieces, you are interested in the slice of pizza, not the cuts. Suppose a pizza is cut into equal size pieces. Calculate the measure of the angle for one slice given the number of pieces.

- **a.** 6 pieces
- **b.** 8 pieces
- **c.** 10 pieces

For Exercises 19–28, find the angle measures. Use the diagram of the protractor below. ∠JVK and ∠KVL are called **adjacent angles** because they have a common vertex and a common side.

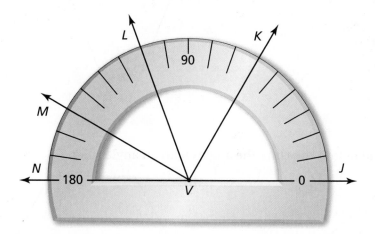

- **19.** $m\angle JVK$
- **20.** $m\angle JVL$
- **21.** $m\angle JVM$
- **22.** $m\angle KVL$
- **23.** $m\angle KVM$
- **24.** $m\angle LVM$
- **25.** the complement of $\angle JVK$
- **26.** the supplement of $\angle JVK$
- **27.** the complement of $\angle MVL$
- **28.** the supplement of $\angle JVL$

29. Without measuring, decide whether the angles in each pair have the same measure. If they do not, tell which angle has the greater measure. Then, find the measure of the angles with an angle ruler or protractor to check your work.

a.

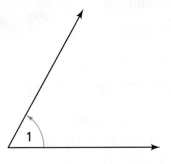 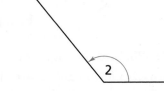

b.

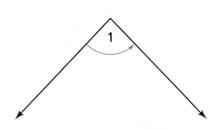 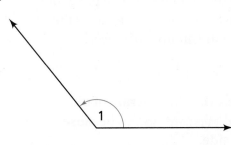

c.

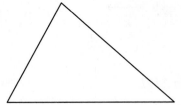 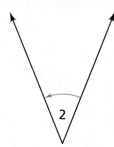

30. For each polygon below, measure the angles with an angle ruler.

a.   **b.**

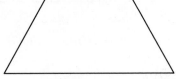

31. Estimate the measure of each angle, then check your answers with an angle ruler or a protractor.

a.

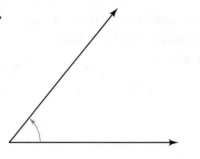

b.

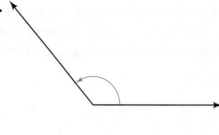

c.

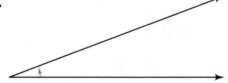

d.

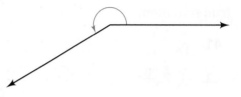

e.

32. Draw an angle for each measure. Include an arc indicating the turn.

  a. 45°

  b. 25°

  c. 180°

  d. 200°

In Exercises 33–36, draw the polygons described. If there is more than one (or no) shape that you can draw, explain how you know that.

33. Draw a rectangle. Perimeter = 24 cm and side of 8 cm.

34. Draw a triangle. Side $\overline{AB}$ = 2 in. Side $\overline{AC}$ = 1 in. $\angle BAC$ = 75°.

35. Draw a triangle. $\angle BAC$ = 75° and $\angle ACB$ = 75°.

36. Draw a trapezoid $PQRS$. $\angle QPS$ = 45°. $\angle RQP$ = 45°. Side $\overline{PS}$ = 1 in. Side $\overline{PQ}$ = 2 in.

Connections

In Exercises 37–40, find two equivalent fractions for each fraction. Find one fraction with a denominator less than the one given. Find another fraction with a denominator greater than the one given.

37. $\frac{4}{12}$

38. $\frac{9}{15}$

39. $\frac{15}{35}$

40. $\frac{20}{12}$

In Exercises 41–44, copy the fractions. Insert $<$, $>$, or $=$ to make a true statement.

41. $\frac{5}{12}$ ■ $\frac{9}{12}$

42. $\frac{15}{35}$ ■ $\frac{12}{20}$

43. $\frac{7}{13}$ ■ $\frac{20}{41}$

44. $\frac{45}{36}$ ■ $\frac{35}{28}$

45. Marissa takes a ride on a merry-go-round. It is shaped like the octagon shown. Marissa's starting point is also shown.

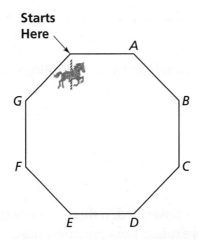

a. **Multiple Choice** Where will Marissa be after the ride completes $\frac{4}{8}$ of a full turn?

   A. point C   **B.** point D

   C. point E   **D.** point G

b. **Multiple Choice** Where will Marissa be after the ride completes $\frac{1}{2}$ of a full turn?

   F. point B   **G.** point C

   H. point D   **J.** point F

46. Multiple Choice Choose the correct statement.

A. $\frac{5}{6} = \frac{11}{360}$

B. $\frac{3}{4} = \frac{300}{360}$

C. $\frac{1}{4} = \frac{90}{360}$

D. $\frac{3}{36} = \frac{33}{360}$

47. The number 360 has many factors. This may be why it was chosen for the number of degrees in a full turn.

a. List all of the factors of 360.

b. Find the prime factorization of 360.

48. You can think of a right angle as one quarter of a complete rotation.

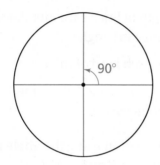

a. How many degrees is $\frac{1}{3}$ of a quarter-rotation?

b. How many degrees is two times a quarter-rotation?

c. How many degrees is two and one third times a quarter-rotation?

For Exercises 49–52, replace the ■ with a number that makes the sentence true.

49. $\frac{1}{2} = \frac{■}{360}$

50. $\frac{1}{10} = \frac{36}{■}$

51. $\frac{1}{■} = \frac{40}{360}$

52. $\frac{■}{3} = \frac{120}{360}$

53. A full turn is 360°. Find the fraction of a turn or number of turns for the given measurement.

a. 90°

b. 270°

c. 720°

d. How many degrees is $\frac{25}{360}$ of a full turn?

54. The minute hand on a watch makes a full rotation each hour. In 30 minutes, the minute hand makes half of a full rotation.

  a. In how many minutes does the hand make $\frac{1}{6}$ of a rotation?

  b. In how many minutes does the hand make $\frac{1}{6}$ of half a rotation?

  c. What fraction of an hour is $\frac{1}{6}$ of half a rotation?

  d. How many degrees has the minute hand moved in $\frac{1}{6}$ of half a rotation?

55. A ruler is used to measure the length of line segments. An angle ruler is used to measure the size of (or turn in) angles.

  a. What is the unit of measure for each kind of ruler?

  b. Compare the method for measuring angles to the method for measuring lines. Use a few sentences.

56. Use the diagram below. Write an equation using the angle measures shown. Then, find the measures of $\angle AVB$ and $\angle BVC$.

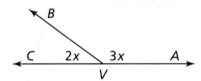

57. Ms. Cosgrove asked her students to estimate the measure of the angle shown.

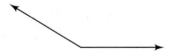

Carly thought 150° would be a good estimate. Hannah said it should be 210°. Who is closer to the exact measurement? Explain.

58. Find the area of the following polygons.

a.

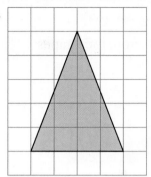

b.

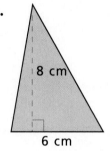

8 cm

6 cm

c.

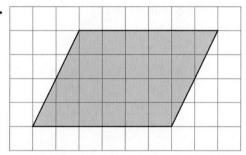

For Exercises 59–63, draw a polygon with the given properties (if possible). Decide if the polygon is unique. If not, design a different second polygon with the same properties.

59. a triangle with a height of 5 cm and a base of 10 cm

60. a triangle with a base of 6 cm and an area of 48 cm

61. a triangle with an area of 12 square centimeters

62. a parallelogram with an area of 24 square centimeters

63. a parallelogram with a height of 4 cm and a base of 8 cm

Extensions

64. Copy and complete the table. Sort the quadrilaterals from the Shapes Set into groups by name and description.

Common Quadrilaterals

Sides and Angles	Name	Examples in the Shapes Set
All sides are the same length.	rhombus	■
All sides are the same length and all angles are right angles.	square	■
All angles are right angles.	rectangle	■
Opposite sides are parallel.	parallelogram	■
Only one pair of opposite sides are parallel.	trapezoid	■

65. Which of the following statements are true? Be able to justify your answers.

  a. All squares are rectangles.

  b. No squares are rhombuses.

  c. All rectangles are parallelograms.

  d. Some rectangles are squares.

  e. Some rectangles are trapezoids.

  f. No trapezoids are parallelograms.

  g. Every quadrilateral is a parallelogram, a trapezoid, a rectangle, a rhombus, or a square.

66. Design a new polar coordinate grid for Four in a Row in Problem 1.2. Play your game with a friend or family member. What ideas did you use to design your new grid? Explain. How does playing on your grid compare to playing on the original grids?

67. A *compass* is a tool used in wilderness navigation. On a compass, *North* is assigned the direction label 0°, *East* is 90°, *South* is 180°, and *West* is 270°. Directions that are between those labels are assigned degree labels such as NE at 45°, for example.

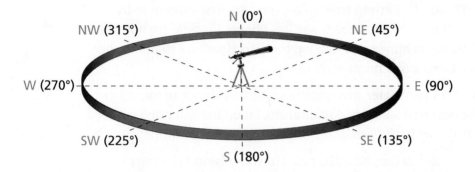

N (0°)
NW (315°)   NE (45°)
W (270°)   E (90°)
SW (225°)   SE (135°)
S (180°)

a. What degree measures would you expect for the direction south-southwest? For north-northwest?

b. A ship at sea is on a heading of 300°. Approximately what direction is it traveling?

68. Major airports label runways with the numbers by the compass heading. For example, a plane on runway 15 is on a compass heading of 150°. A plane on runway 9 is on a compass heading of 90°.

a. What is the runway number of a plane that is taking off on a heading due west? On a heading due east?

b. What is the compass heading of a plane landing on runway 6? On runway 12?

c. Each actual runway has two direction labels. The label depends on the direction in which a landing or taking off plane is headed. How are those labels related to each other?

69. When you and your classmates measure an angle, you have found
that your measurements are slightly different. No measuring tool is
absolutely precise, so there is a little error in every measurement. For
example, when using angle measures to navigate an airplane, even
small errors can lead a flight far astray.

In 1937, Amelia Earhart tried to become the first woman to fly
around the world. On June 1, she left Miami, Florida. On July 2, she
left Lae, New Guinea and headed towards Howland Island in the
Pacific Ocean. She never arrived.

In 2012, 75 years later, investigators found evidence of the crash
on the deserted island of Nikumaroro, far off her intended course.
An error may have been made in plotting Earhart's course.

The map shows Lae, New Guinea; Howland Island (Earhart's
intended destination); and Nikumaroro Island (the crash site).

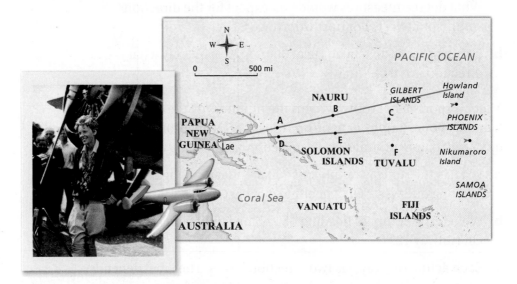

a. How many degrees off course was Earhart's crash site from her
intended destination?

b. Suppose two planes fly along the paths formed by the rays of the
angle indicated on the map. Both planes leave Lae, New Guinea,
at the same time. They fly at the same speed. Use the scale in
the upper left corner of the map. Find the distance between
the planes at each pair of points labeled on the map (A and D,
B and E, and C and F).

c. Amelia Earhart apparently flew several degrees south of her
intended course. Suppose you start at New Guinea and are trying
to reach Howland, but you fly 20° south. On which island might
you land?

In this Investigation, you developed an understanding of the family of polygon shapes and angles that describe rotations or change of direction. You learned how to estimate angle measures and use tools to make more precise measurements. You also learned how to draw geometric shapes from a given list of properties. The following questions will help you summarize what you have learned.

Think about these questions. Discuss your ideas with other students and your teacher. Then write a summary of your findings in your notebook.

1. **What** are the common properties of all polygons?

2. **What** does the measure in degrees tell you about an angle? **What** are some common benchmark angles?

3. **What** strategies can be used to estimate angle measures? To deduce angle measures from given information? To find accurate measurements with tools?

Unit Project

At the end of this Unit, you will create a special report, a poster, a work of art, or a slide presentation. Your project will demonstrate what you learned about the properties and uses of polygons.

 What ideas from this Investigation seem important or attractive to include in your presentation?

Common Core Mathematical Practices

As you worked on the Problems in this Investigation, you used prior knowledge to make sense of them. You also applied Mathematical Practices to solve the Problems. Think back over your work, the ways you thought about the Problems, and how you used Mathematical Practices.

Ken described his thoughts in the following way:

> When working Problem 1.5, Sam thought that there was only one possible triangle that could have a base of 2 units and a height of 1 unit. Sam's example was a right triangle.
>
> But, Ali showed that the height does not have to be a side of the triangle. So, we could make a whole family of triangles that have a base of 2 units and a height of 1 unit.
>
> ....
>
> **Common Core Standards for Mathematical Practice**
>
> **MP3** Construct viable arguments and critique the reasoning of others.

• What other Mathematical Practices can you identify in Ken's reasoning?

• Describe a Mathematical Practice that you and your classmates used to solve a different Problem in this Investigation.

Investigation 2

Designing Polygons: The Angle Connection

This Investigation develops properties of polygons. These properties make polygons useful in many natural objects like the combs made by bees to store their honey.

2.1 Angle Sums of Regular Polygons

You have seen that polygons with the same number of sides can have different shapes. However, there is an important relationship between the number of sides and the angle sum of any polygon. You will develop a formula that relates the number of sides to angle measures.

A **regular polygon** is a polygon in which all of the sides are the same length and all of the angles have the same measure. In an **irregular polygon,** not all of the sides are the same length or not all of the angles have the same measure.

Polygons are named based on the number of sides and angles they have. For example, a polygon with six sides and six angles is called a *hexagon*.

Common Core State Standards

7.EE.A.2 Understand that rewriting an expression in different forms in a problem context can shed light on the problem and how the quantities in it are related.

7.EE.B.4 Use variables to represent quantities in a real world or mathematical problem, and construct simple equations . . . to solve problems by reasoning about the quantities.

Below are six examples of polygons from the Shapes Set. Study these examples to find a relationship between the number of sides and angles.

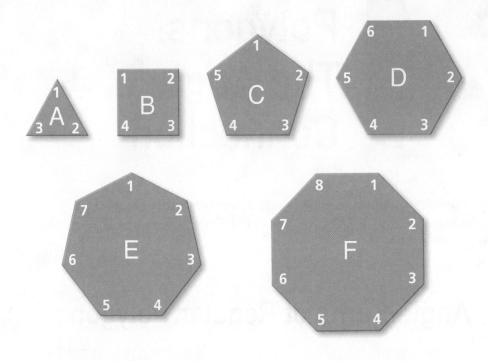

? Is there a relationship between the size of the angles and the number of sides for regular polygons?

Problem 2.1

You can discover relationships between the number of sides and the angle measures of polygons. Measure some examples, organize the data, and then look for patterns.

A Use an angle ruler to measure the angles in the equilateral triangle, the square, the regular pentagon, and the regular hexagon from the Shapes Set.

1. Enter the results in a table like that begun here.

Polygon	Number of Sides	Measure of an Angle	Angle Sum
Triangle	■	■	■
Square	■	■	■
Pentagon	■	■	■
Hexagon	■	■	■
Heptagon	■	■	■
Octagon	■	■	■
Nonagon	■	■	■
Decagon	■	■	■

2. Find a pattern that suggests a way to fill in the table for regular polygons with seven, eight, nine, and ten sides. Then measure the angles of the Shapes Set heptagon and octagon. See if your pattern holds in those cases.

3. Describe a pattern relating angle sums to number of sides in regular polygons.

4. Describe a pattern relating measures of individual angles and number of sides in regular polygons.

continued on the next page >

Problem **2.1** *continued*

B The diagram below shows two sets of regular polygons of different sizes. Does the pattern relating number of sides, measures of angles, and angle sums apply to all of these shapes? Explain your reasoning.

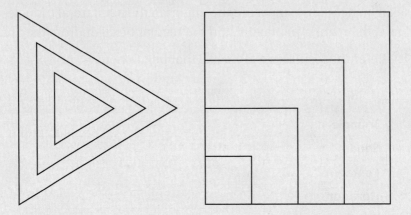

C Explain how you could find the angle sum of a regular polygon with *n* sides. Then, write your conjecture as a formula $S = $ _____. The right side of the equation should give an expression for calculating the sum from the value of *n*.

D Explain how you could find the measure of each angle in a regular polygon with *n* sides. Then, write your conjecture as a formula $A = $ _____. The right side of the equation should give an expression for calculating the measure of each angle from the value of *n*.

ACE Homework starts on page 52.

2.2 Angle Sums of Any Polygon

Does the pattern you observed in angle sums of regular polygons apply to irregular polygons? To tackle this question, you could draw many different polygons and measure all of the angles. But there are other strategies that provide answers with a little experimentation and some careful thinking.

Problem 2.2

Devon, Trevor, and Casey tried three different ways to find a formula relating the angle sum of any polygon to the number of sides.

A Devon began by drawing irregular triangles and quadrilaterals. Then he tore the corners off of those polygons and 'added' the angles by arranging them like this:

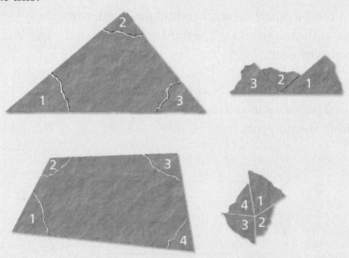

1. What angle sum does Devon's work suggest for the triangle? For the quadrilateral?

2. Test Devon's idea with triangles and quadrilaterals of your own design. See if you get the same result.

3. Draw irregular pentagons and hexagons. Use Devon's method to determine the angle sums for those figures.

4. Does this 'draw and tear' experimentation show the same angle sum pattern that you discovered with regular polygons? Why or why not?

continued on the next page >

$\mathcal{P}roblem$ **2.2** $continued$

B Trevor examined Devon's results from his study of irregular triangles. This gave him a new idea to study polygons with more sides. He divided some polygons into smaller triangles by drawing diagonals from one vertex.

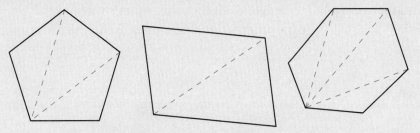

1. Describe the relationship between the number of sides of a polygon and the number of triangles formed.

2. Find the angle sum of each polygon. It might help to use Trevor's drawings and what you learned earlier about the angle sum of any triangle.

3. Will Trevor's method work to find the angle sum of any polygon? If so, what equation would relate the angle sum S to the number of sides n? If not, why not?

C Casey used Devon's discovery about triangles in a different way. She divided polygons into triangles by drawing line segments from a point within the polygon.

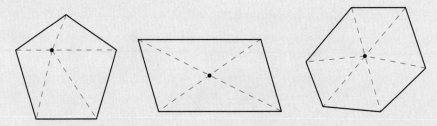

1. Study Casey's drawings to find the angle sum of each polygon.

2. Will Casey's method work to find the angle sum of any polygon? If so, what pattern would relate the angle sum S to the number of sides n? If not, why not?

D Think about your experimentation and reasoning about irregular polygons. Did you produce an angle sum pattern that agrees with what you found for regular polygons? Explain.

A C E Homework starts on page 52.

2.3 The Bees Do It
Polygons in Nature

Honeybees build nests called hives. A typical hive might be home for as many as 60,000 bees. Bees are small insects, but packing a hive with that many bees and the honey they make is tricky.

The honey is stored in a comb filled with tubes. The tops of those tubes cover the comb with a pattern of identical regular hexagons.

- Why do the bees form their honey storage tubes in the shape of hexagonal prisms?

- Why not some other shape?

The diagram below shows a pattern that uses regular hexagons to cover a flat surface without any gaps or overlaps.

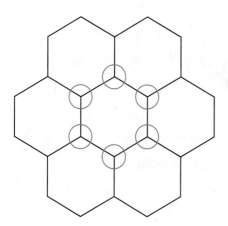

Notice that three angles fit together exactly around any point in the beehive pattern. These patterns are called **tilings** or **tessellations** of the surface.

 What other regular polygons do you think can be used to tile a surface?

Problem 2.3

Use regular polygons from the Shapes Set to explore possibilities for covering a flat surface with polygon tiles. Then, use what you know about the angles of regular polygons to explain your discoveries.

A Which regular polygons from the Shapes Set can be used to cover a flat surface without gaps or overlap like the hexagon pattern shown on the previous page?

- Sketch any tilings that you discover.

- Explain why copies of the shape fit neatly around the points where they meet.

B Which regular polygons from the Shapes Set cannot be used to cover a flat surface without gaps or overlap? Explain why.

C Think about tiling with regular polygons that have more than eight sides.

  1. How do the angle sizes change as the number of sides increases?

  2. Do you think any regular polygons of 9, 10, 11, or 12 sides could be used to tile a flat surface? Why or why not?

D Most regular polygons cannot be used to tile flat surfaces. However, it is often possible to include them in tilings that use two or more shapes.

  1. Find and sketch tilings with two or more polygons from the Shapes Set.

  2. What do you observe about angles that meet at a point in mixed tilings?

A C E Homework starts on page 52.

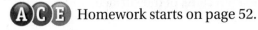

Did You Know?

A golf ball manufacturer developed a hexagon pattern for the cover of golf balls. They claim it is the first design to cover 100% of the surface area of a ball. This pattern of mostly hexagons almost eliminates flat spots that interfere with performance. The new design produces a longer, better flight for the golf ball.

2.4 The Ins and Outs of Polygons

Familiar figures like triangles, parallelograms, and trapezoids are called
convex polygons. Figures like the star and the arrowhead pictured here
are called **concave polygons.**

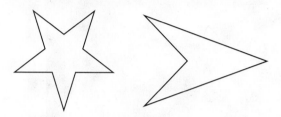

For convex polygons it is clear which points are on the inside and which
are on the outside. It is also clear how to measure the **interior angles.**

By extending a side of a convex polygon, you can make an **exterior angle**
that lies outside the polygon.

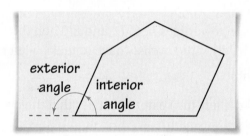

The figures below show two ways to form exterior angles. You can extend
the sides as you move in either direction around the polygon.

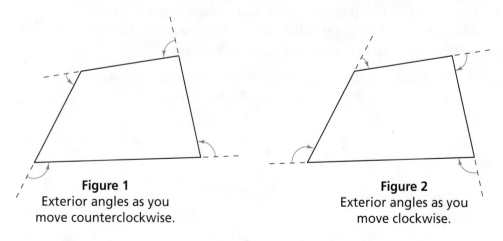

Figure 1
Exterior angles as you
move counterclockwise.

Figure 2
Exterior angles as you
move clockwise.

Measuring exterior angles provides useful information about the interior
angles of a polygon.

Problem 2.4

Members of the Columbia Triathlon Club train by bicycling around the polygonal path shown.

They start at vertex *A* and go on to vertices *B*, *C*, *D*, and *E*. Then they return to *A* and start another lap. At each vertex the cyclists have to make a left turn through an *exterior angle* of the polygon.

A **1.** What is the sum of the left-turn exterior angles that the cyclists make on one full lap around this path?

  • Explain how you can arrive at an answer without measuring.

  • Then, measure the exterior angles to check your thinking.

2. Draw several other polygons. Include a triangle, a quadrilateral, and a hexagon. Find the sums of the turn angles if you cycle around each figure and return to your start point and direction.

3. Will the turning pattern you observed in cycling around several polygons occur in any other polygons? Why or why not?

Problem **2.4** *continued*

Each exterior angle and its adjacent interior angle are *supplementary angles*.

B **1.** Consider the polygonal training track shown on the previous page. How many pairs of supplementary angles are there?

2. Amy says there are 5 straight angles in the diagram. They total $T = 5 \cdot 180°$. She thinks there is way to figure out the part of T that is the sum of the interior angles. She also wants the part of T that is the sum of the exterior angles. How can she find each part of T?

3. Becky says $T = n \times 180°$ should work for the total of exterior and interior angles for any polygon. So $n \times 180° - 360°$ should give her the sum of the interior angles of any polygon. But this does not look like the formula she found in Problem 2.2. Use the formula you developed in Problem 2.2. Explain to Becky why her formula is equivalent.

C Nic thought about exterior angles and 'walking around' a polygon. He came up with a new way to prove that the sum of the interior angles of any triangle is 180°. Answer Nic's questions that follow to complete his proof.

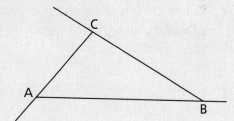

1. What is the sum of all of the interior and exterior angles in any triangle?

2. What is the sum of the exterior angles?

3. How much is left for the sum of the interior angles?

D For each of the following triangles write and solve an equation to find the value of *x*. Use the results to find the size of each angle. Find the supplement of each interior angle.

1.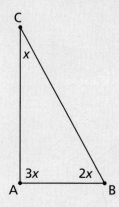

2.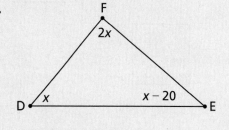

ACE Homework starts on page 52.

Applications

1. Without measuring, find the measure of the angle labeled *x* in each regular polygon.

   a.
   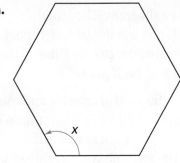

   b.
   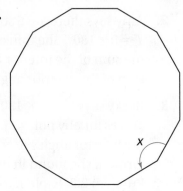

2. Below are sets of regular polygons of different sizes. Does the length of a side of a regular polygon affect the sum of the interior angle measures? Explain.

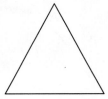

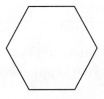

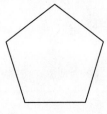

For Exercises 3–10, find the measure of each angle labeled *x*.

3.
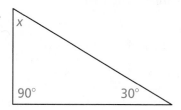

4.
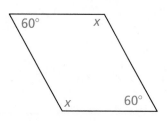

5.
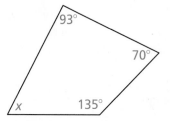

6.
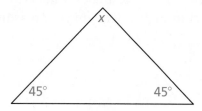

7.
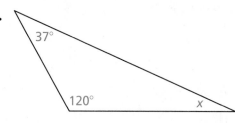

8. This figure is a regular hexagon.

9. This figure is a parallelogram.
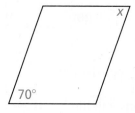

10. This figure is a trapezoid.
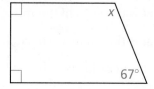

11. A right triangle has one right angle and two acute angles. Without measuring the angles, what is the sum of the measures of the two acute angles? Explain your reasoning.

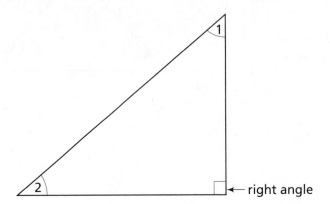

2   right angle

12. The figure below is a regular dodecagon. It has 12 sides.

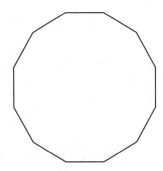

   a. What is the sum of the measures of the angles of this polygon?

   b. What is the measure of each angle?

   c. Can copies of this polygon be used to tile a flat surface? Explain.

13. Multiple Choice Which of the following combinations will tile a flat surface?

   A. regular heptagons and equilateral triangles

   B. squares and regular octagons

   C. regular pentagons and regular hexagons

   D. regular hexagons and squares

14. Suppose in-line skaters make one complete lap around a park shaped like the quadrilateral below.

What is the sum of the angles through which they turn?

15. Suppose the skaters complete one lap around a park that has the shape of a regular pentagon.

a. What is the sum of the angles through which they turn?

b. How many degrees will the skaters turn if they go once around a regular hexagon? A regular octagon? A regular polygon with *n* sides? Explain.

Connections

16. The regular decagon and star below are ten-sided polygons.

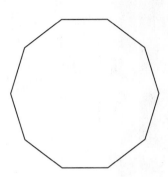

    a. Measure the angles inside the star to find the angle sum of the star.

    b. Calculate the interior angle sum for a regular decagon and compare it to your measured sum for the star.

    c. Use a strategy like that of Casey's to split the star into triangles. That is, draw lines from the center of rotation to each vertex of the star. Use that diagram to calculate the sum of angles for the star.

    d. Explain why your result in part (c) does or does not match the measurements in part (a).

17. The diagram shows a line of symmetry for an equilateral triangle.

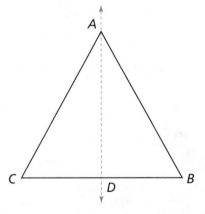

Examine the two smaller triangles that are formed using a part of the symmetry line. What do you know about the angles and the line segments of triangles *ABD* and *ACD*? Give reasons to support your answers.

18. **Multiple Choice** Figure QSTV is a rectangle. The lengths QR and QV are equal. What is the measure of angle x?

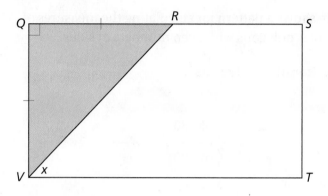

    F. $20°$ **G.** $45°$ **H.** $90°$ **J.** $120°$

19. Choose a non-rectangular parallelogram from the Shapes Set or draw one of your own. Using copies of your parallelogram, can you make a tiling pattern? Sketch a picture to help explain what you found.

20. Choose a scalene triangle (all three sides of different lengths) from your Shapes Set or draw one of your own. Using copies of your scalene triangle, can you make a tiling pattern? Sketch a picture to help explain what you found.

21. A class was asked what convinced them that the sum of exterior angles in any polygon is 360°. Here are three different points of view.

> "We were convinced when we drew a bunch of different figures and used my angle ruler to measure the exterior angles. They all came out close to 360°."

> "We were convinced when we thought about walking around the figure and realized that we made one complete turn or 360°."

> "We used the results about sums of interior angles and the fact that the measure of each interior angle plus its adjacent exterior angle is 180° to deduce the formula using algebra."

What are the pros and cons of each argument?

Extensions

22. The table begun here shows a pattern for calculating the measures of interior angles in regular polygons with even numbers of sides.

Regular Polygons

Number of Sides	Measure of Interior Angle
4	$\frac{1}{2}$ of 180°
6	$\frac{2}{3}$ of 180°
8	$\frac{3}{4}$ of 180°
10	▪
12	▪

a. What entry would give the angle measures for decagons and dodecagons? Are those entries correct? How do you know?

b. Is there a similar pattern for regular polygons with odd numbers of sides? If so, what is the pattern?

23. Kele claims that the angle sum of a polygon he has drawn is 1660°. Can he be correct? Explain.

24. Look at the polygons below. Does Trevor's method of finding the angle sum (Problem 2.2) still work? Does Casey's method still work? Can you still find the angle sum of the interior angles without measuring? Explain.

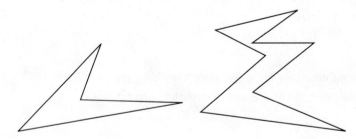

25. Below are a quadrilateral and a pentagon with the diagonals drawn from all of the vertices.

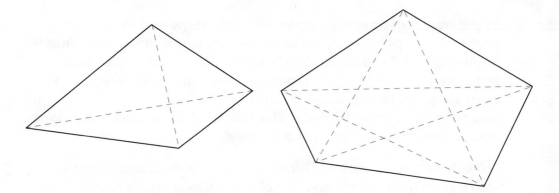

a. How many diagonals does the quadrilateral have? How many diagonals does the pentagon have?

b. Find the total number of diagonals for a hexagon and for a heptagon.

c. Copy the table below and record your results from parts (a) and (b).

Number of Sides	4	5	6	7	8	9	10	11	12
Number of Diagonals	■	■	■	■	■	■	■	■	■

Look for a pattern relating the number of sides and the number of diagonals. Complete the table.

d. Write a rule for finding the number of diagonals for a polygon with *n* sides.

In this Investigation, you explored angle sums and tiling properties of polygons. You also used facts about supplementary angles to write and solve simple equations about angles in a polygon. In developing formulas for angle sums of polygons, you used variables to represent quantities in a mathematical problem and to construct the formula. The following questions will help you summarize what you have learned.

Think about these questions. Discuss your ideas with other students and your teacher. Then write a summary of your findings in your notebook.

1. **How** is the number of sides related to the sum of the interior angles in a polygon? **What** about the sum of the exterior angles?

2. **How** is the measure of each interior angle related to the number of sides in a regular polygon? **What** about the measure of each exterior angle?

3. **Which** polygons can be used to tile a flat surface without overlaps or gaps? **Why** are those the only figures that work as tiles?

Unit Project

Think about the discoveries from your work on the Problems in this Investigation.

 What seems worthy of including in a report, poster, or presentation about the *Shapes and Designs* Unit?

Common Core Mathematical Practices

As you worked on the Problems in this Investigation, you used prior knowledge to make sense of them. You also applied Mathematical Practices to solve the Problems. Think back over your work, the ways you thought about the Problems, and how you used Mathematical Practices.

Shawna described her thoughts in the following way:

> When completing the table in Problem 2.1, we noticed there was a relationship between the number of sides of a regular polygon and the measure of each angle.
>
> We recognized a pattern in our table and were able to use it to fill in the table for polygons with seven, eight, nine, and ten sides. Then, we wrote a formula to find the measure of each angle for any regular polygon with *n* sides.
>
> ....
>
> **Common Core Standards for Mathematical Practice**
>
> **MP8** Look for and express regularity in repeated reasoning.

- What other Mathematical Practices can you identify in Shawna's reasoning?
- Describe a Mathematical Practice that you and your classmates used to solve a different Problem in this Investigation.

3

Designing Triangles and Quadrilaterals

Your work on Problems in Investigation 2 revealed properties of polygons that make them useful in natural objects like the honeycombs made by bees. In this Investigation you will discover properties of polygons that make them useful in buildings, mechanical devices, and crafts.

To explore the connections between shapes and their uses in construction, you will build some polygons using polystrips and fasteners like these.

These tools will allow you to build and study polygons with various combinations of side lengths and angles.

Common Core State Standards

7.G.A.2 Draw (freehand, with ruler and protractor, and with technology) geometric shapes with given conditions. Focus on constructing triangles from three measures of angles or sides, noticing when the conditions determine a unique triangle, more than one triangle, or no triangle.

7.G.B.5 Use facts about supplementary, complementary, vertical, and adjacent angles in a multi-step problem to write and solve simple equations for an unknown angle in a figure.

3.1 Building Triangles

Bridges, towers, and other structures contain many triangles in their design.

- What properties of these simple polygons could make them valuable in construction?

Problem 3.1

The best way to discover what is so special about triangles in construction is to build several models and study their reaction to pressure.

A Make and study several test triangles using the steps below. Sketch and label your results.

Step 1 Pick three numbers between 2 and 20 for side lengths of a polystrip triangle.

Step 2 Try to make a triangle with the chosen side lengths. If you can build a triangle, try to build a different triangle with the same side lengths.

Repeat Steps 1 and 2 to make and study several other triangles. Record your results in a table with headings like this

Side Lengths	Triangle Possible?	Sketch	Different Shape?
■	■	■	■

1. List some sets of side lengths that did make a triangle.

2. List some sets of side lengths that did not make a triangle.

B Study your results from Question A with different side length possibilities.

1. What pattern do you see that explains why some sets of numbers make a triangle and some do not?

2. For what side length relationships can you make more than one triangle from a given set of side lengths?

3. Find three other side lengths that make a triangle. Then, find three other side lengths that will not make a triangle.

ACE Homework starts on page 76.

3.2 Design Challenge II
Drawing Triangles

▶ The drawing here shows a triangle with measures of all angles and sides.

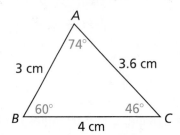

? Suppose you want to text a friend to give directions for drawing an exact copy of the figure. What is the shortest message to do the job? How do you know?

Problem 3.2

To find an answer to the challenge of describing triangles in only a few words, work through this Problem.

Ⓐ Which of these short messages give enough information to draw a triangle congruent to △*ABC* above?

1. $\overline{BC}$ = 4 cm
$\angle B$ = 60°
$\overline{AB}$ = 3 cm

2. $\angle B$ = 60°
$\overline{BC}$ = 4 cm
$\angle C$ = 46°

3. $\overline{AB}$ = 3 cm
$\overline{BC}$ = 4 cm
$\angle C$ = 46°

4. $\angle B$ = 60°
$\angle A$ = 74°
$\angle C$ = 46°

5. $\angle B$ = 60°
$\angle C$ = 46°
$\overline{AC}$ = 3.6 cm

Problem **3.2**   *continued*

B Write the shortest possible messages that tell how to draw triangles with the same size and shape as the ones below.

1.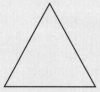

2.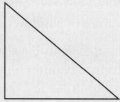

3.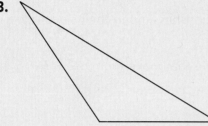

4.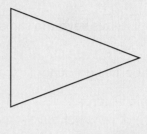

C What minimum information about a triangle allows you to draw exactly one triangle?

D Draw a triangle *ABC* in which angle *B* measures 90°. Then make a copy using the same three lengths of sides. Is your copy also a right triangle? Does it matter in what order you connect the sides?

A C E Homework starts on page 76.

3.3 Building Quadrilaterals

Quadrilaterals, especially rectangles, appear throughout buildings in which we live, work, and go to school. You see rectangles as the mortar around bricks, the frames of windows, and the outlines of large buildings.

Most buildings stand up because of a rectangular frame of studs and beams. Rectangles have very different physical properties from triangles.

- Do quadrilaterals have the same relationship among their sides as triangles?

- What properties do quadrilaterals have that make them useful?

Problem 3.3

Your study of triangle properties will help you understand quadrilaterals. You will use polystrips to build and test some sample quadrilaterals.

A Build polystrip quadrilaterals with each of the following sets of numbers as side lengths. If you are able to build one quadrilateral with a set of side lengths, try to build two or more different figures using those side lengths. Sketch and label your results.

1. 6, 10, 15, 15

2. 3, 5, 10, 20

3. 8, 8, 10, 10

4. 12, 20, 6, 9

B Choose your own set of four numbers. Use them as side lengths to try to build quadrilaterals. Record your results. Combine your results with your observations from Question A.

1. Is it possible to make a quadrilateral using any set of four side lengths? If not, how can you tell when you can make a quadrilateral from four side lengths?

2. Can you make two or more different quadrilaterals from the same four side lengths?

3. What combinations of side lengths are needed to build rectangles? Squares? Parallelograms?

Problem 3.3 *continued*

C Use several of your polystrip figures to study the reaction of triangles and quadrilaterals to stress.

1. Hold one of your triangles and push down on a vertex. What happens?

   This stress test is similar to the way a bridge would act under the weight of a car or a train.

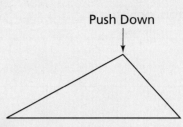
Push Down

2. What happens when you push down on a side or vertex of a quadrilateral?

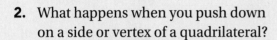
Push Down

3. How do the results from your stress tests in parts (1) and (2) explain the frequent use of triangles in building structures ike bridges and towers?

D Use a polystrip to add a diagonal to a test quadrilateral from Question C, part (2).

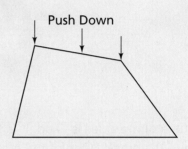

Repeat the same stress test from Question C, part (2). Does your quadrilateral respond differently? If so, why do you think there is a different response with an additional diagonal brace?

E Describe what you learned from experiments in building triangles and quadrilaterals. How are the two kinds of polygons similar and different? How do the differences explain the frequent use of triangles when building structures?

A C E Homework starts on page 76.

Did You Know?

Mechanical engineers use the fact that quadrilaterals are not rigid figures to design *linkages*. Here is an example of a quadrilateral linkage made from polystrips.

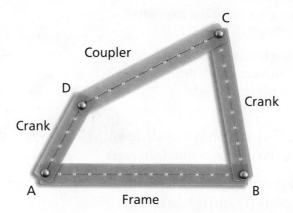

One of the sides is fixed. It is the *frame*. The two sides attached to the frame are the *cranks*. One of the cranks is the driver and the other the follower. The fourth side is called the *coupler*. Quadrilateral linkages are used for windshield wipers, automobile jacks, and reclining lawn chairs.

In 1883, the German mathematician Franz Grashof suggested an interesting principle for quadrilateral linkages. Sum the lengths of the shortest and longest sides. If that sum is less than or equal to the sum of the other two sides, then the shortest side can rotate 360°.

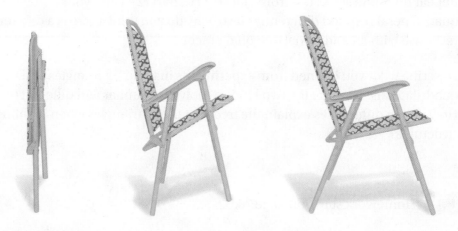

3.4 Parallel Lines and Transversals

Suppose you were asked to build a quadrilateral with side lengths 3, 8, 3, and 8. You might expect that the figure is a 3 × 8 rectangle. Your experiments in Problem 3.3 showed that when you push on a vertex of a polystrip rectangle, it loses its square-corner shape.

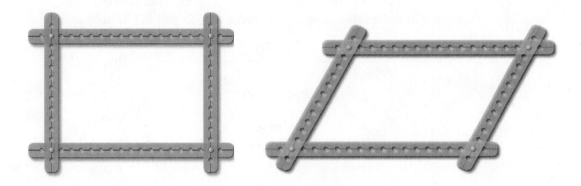

One thing that does not change about the polystrip figure is the relationship of the opposite sides. They remain equal in length and parallel to each other.

Parallel lines are lines in a plane that never meet. They are like railroad tracks, rows of a crop in a field, or lines on notebook paper. They remain the same distance apart and never meet, even if extended forever in both directions.

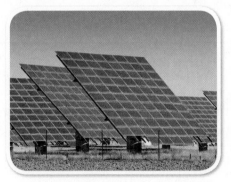

A **parallelogram** is a quadrilateral in which the pairs of opposite sides are parallel. The shape of a parallelogram is largely set by the angles at which those pairs of sides meet. A parallelogram with four right angles is a **rectangle.**

Problem 3.4

A There are nine parallelograms in the Shapes Set from Problem 1.1.

1. What pattern seems to relate the measures of opposite angles in any parallelogram?

2. What pattern seems to relate the measures of consecutive angles in any parallelogram?

3. Suppose your conjectures in parts (1) and (2) are true. What are the measures of the angles in parallelograms *ABCD* and *JKLM* below?

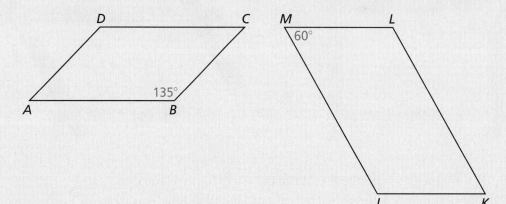

B Suppose your conjectures from Question A are true. The lines below form a parallelogram.

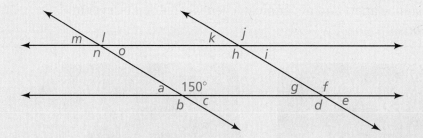

Find the measures of all labeled angles in this diagram. Be prepared to justify each answer.

Problem 3.4 *continued*

C A line that intersects two other lines is called a **transversal.**

    1. From your work in Questions A and B, what can you say about the measures of the eight angles formed by a transversal and two parallel lines?

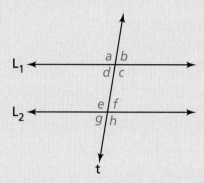

    2. Suppose the measure of angle *f* is 80°. What are the measures of the other labeled angles?

D You probably noticed that when two lines intersect four angles are formed. The opposite pairs of angles are called **vertical angles.** For example, in Question C, angles *f* and *g* are vertical angles.

    1. Name the other pairs of vertical angles in the figure of Question C.

    2. Name the pairs of supplementary angles in that figure.

    3. What is true about the measures of any vertical angle pair? Explain how you know.

E Use what you know about complementary, supplementary, and vertical angles. Write an equation and then find the value of *x* and the size of each angle in this figure.

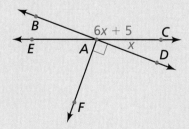

ACE Homework starts on page 76.

3.5 Design Challenge III
The Quadrilateral Game

Special properties of triangles and quadrilaterals make them useful in the design of buildings and mechanical objects. They also play an important role in the design of craft objects.

The two common forms of **symmetry** are defined below.

Reflectional Symmetry

A shape with reflectional symmetry has halves that are mirror images of each other.

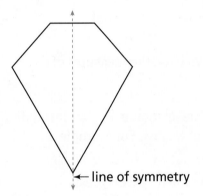

If you fold along the line of symmetry, the two halves of the figure match exactly. If you hold a mirror along the line of symmetry, the figure's reflection will match the half behind the mirror.

Rotational Symmetry

A shape with rotational symmetry can be turned about a center point through some angle between 0° and 360° and it will look the same.

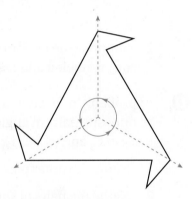

If you close your eyes as the figure above is rotated 120° or 240° and then open them, you won't notice any difference.

Problem 3.5

A Spotting symmetries in polygons is the first step in using those figures to make art and craft designs.

1. What kind of symmetries do the triangles in the Shapes Set have?

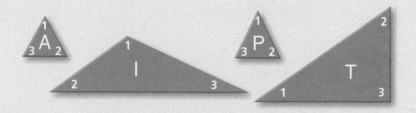

2. What kind of symmetries do the quadrilaterals in the Shapes Set have?

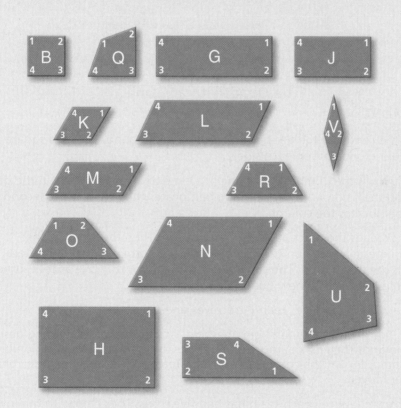

3. Look for objects in your classroom or in nature that have symmetries. What kind of symmetries do they have?

continued on the next page >

Problem **3.5** *continued*

The Quadrilateral Game challenges you to use all that you know about polygons, including symmetry. The game is played by two teams. To play, you need two number cubes, a game grid, a geoboard, and a rubber band.

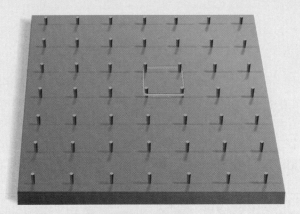

The Quadrilateral Game

Directions

- Near the center of the geoboard, put the rubber band around a square measuring one unit on each side.

- Team A rolls the number cubes one at a time to locate an entry in the game grid on the next page. The first number locates the row and the second number locates the column.

- Team A reads the description in that location. Then they look at the quadrilateral already on the game board, and form a new quadrilateral to match the description. The challenge for Team A is to move as few corners as possible to make the new quadrilateral.

- For each corner moved, Team A receives one point.

- Next, Team B rolls the number cubes and locates the corresponding description on the grid. They make a quadrilateral matching the new description by moving as few of the corners as possible. Team B receives one point for each corner moved.

- Play continues until each team has had five turns. The team with the lowest score at the end is the winner.

Problem **3.5** *continued*

B Play the Quadrilateral Game. Keep a record of interesting strategies and difficult situations.

1. When did you receive 0 points during a turn? Why didn't you need to move any corners on those turns?

2. Write two new descriptions of quadrilaterals that you could use in the game grid.

3. Make your own game board with descriptions for a Triangle Game.

Quadrilateral Game Grid

	Column 1	Column 2	Column 3	Column 4	Column 5	Column 6
Row 6	A quadrilateral that is a square	**Add 1 point to your score and skip your turn**	A rectangle that is not a square	A quadrilateral with two obtuse angles	A quadrilateral with exactly one pair of parallel sides	A quadrilateral with one pair of opposite side lengths equal
Row 5	**Subtract 2 points from your score and skip your turn**	A quadrilateral that is not a rectangle	A quadrilateral with two pairs of consecutive angles that are equal	A quadrilateral with all four angles the same size	A quadrilateral with four lines of symmetry	A quadrilateral that is a rectangle
Row 4	A quadrilateral with no reflectional or rotational symmetry	A quadrilateral with four right angles	**Skip a turn**	A quadrilateral with exactly one pair of consecutive side lengths that are equal	A quadrilateral with exactly one right angle	A quadrilateral with two 45° angles
Row 3	A quadrilateral with no angles equal	A quadrilateral with one pair of equal opposite angles	A quadrilateral with exactly one pair of opposite angles that are equal	**Add 2 points to your score and skip your turn**	A quadrilateral with no sides parallel	A quadrilateral with exactly two right angles
Row 2	A quadrilateral with both pairs of adjacent side lengths equal	A quadrilateral with two pairs of equal opposite angles	A quadrilateral with a diagonal that divides it into two identical shapes	A quadrilateral that is a rhombus	A quadrilateral with 180° rotational symmetry	**Subtract 1 point from your score and skip your turn**
Row 1	A quadrilateral with one diagonal that is a line of symmetry	A quadrilateral with no side lengths equal	A quadrilateral with exactly one angle greater than 180°	A parallelogram that is not a rectangle	**Add 3 points to your score and skip your turn**	A quadrilateral with two pairs of opposite side lengths equal

A C E Homework starts on page 76.

Applications

For Exercises 1–4, follow these directions. Use the given side lengths.

- If possible, build a triangle with the side lengths. Sketch your triangle.
- Tell whether your triangle is the only one that is possible. Explain.
- If a triangle is not possible, explain why.

1. 5, 5, 3

2. 8, 8, 8

3. 7, 8, 15

4. 5, 6, 10

5. From Exercises 1–4, which sets of side lengths can make each of the following shapes?

    a. an equilateral triangle (all three sides are equal length)

    b. an isosceles triangle (two sides are equal length)

    c. a scalene triangle (no two sides are equal length)

    d. a triangle with at least two angles of the same measure

For Exercises 6 and 7, draw the polygons described to help you answer the questions.

6. Suppose you want to build a triangle with three angles measuring 60°. What do you think must be true of the side lengths? What kind of triangle is this?

7. Suppose you want to build a triangle with only two angles the same size. What do you think must be true of the side lengths? What kind of triangle is this?

8. Giraldo is building a tent. He has two 3-foot poles. He also has a 5-foot pole, a 6-foot pole, and a 7-foot pole. He wants to make a triangular-shaped doorframe for the tent using the 3-foot poles and one other pole. Which of the other poles could be used for the base of the door?

9. Which of these descriptions of a triangle *ABC* are directions that can be followed to draw exactly one shape?

  a. $\overline{AB} = 2.5$ in., $\overline{AC} = 2$ in., $\angle B = 40°$

  b. $\overline{AB} = 2.5$ in., $\overline{AC} = 1$ in., $\angle A = 40°$

  c. $\overline{AB} = 2.5$ in., $\angle B = 60°$, $\angle A = 40°$

  d. $\overline{AB} = 2.5$ in., $\angle B = 60°$, $\angle A = 130°$

For Exercises 10–13, follow these directions. Use the given side lengths.

• If possible, build a quadrilateral with the side lengths. Sketch your quadrilateral.

• Tell whether your quadrilateral is the only one that is possible. Explain.

• If a quadrilateral is not possible, explain why.

10. 5, 5, 8, 8   **11.** 5, 5, 6, 14

12. 8, 8, 8, 8   **13.** 4, 3, 5, 14

14. From Exercises 10–13, which sets of side lengths can make each of the following shapes?

  a. a square   **b.** a quadrilateral with all angles the same size

  c. a parallelogram   **d.** a quadrilateral that is not a parallelogram

15. A quadrilateral with four equal sides is called a *rhombus*. Which set(s) of side lengths from Exercises 10–13 can make a rhombus?

16. A quadrilateral with just one pair of parallel sides is called a *trapezoid*. Which sets of side lengths from Exercises 10–13 can make a trapezoid?

17. In the diagram below, line *T* is a transversal to parallel lines L_1 and L_2.

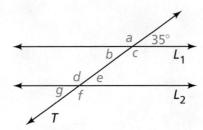

   a. Find the degree measures of angles labeled *a–g*.

   b. Name the pairs of opposite or vertical angles in the figure.

18. Which of these shapes have reflectional symmetry? Which of these shapes have rotational symmetry?

Multiple Choice For Exercises 19–22, choose the symmetry or symmetries of each shape.

  19. rhombus (four equal sides)

     A. rotation   **B.** reflection   **C.** both A and B   **D.** none

  20. regular pentagon

     F. rotation   **G.** reflection   **H.** both F and G   **J.** none

  21. square

     A. rotation   **B.** reflection   **C.** both A and B   **D.** none

  22. parallelogram (not a rhombus or a rectangle)

     F. rotation   **G.** reflection   **H.** both F and G   **J.** none

For Exercises 23 and 24, draw the polygons described to help you answer the questions.

23. To build a square, what must be true of the side lengths?

24. Suppose you want to build a rectangle that is not a square. What must be true of the side lengths?

25. Li Mei builds a quadrilateral with sides that are each five inches long. To help stabilize the quadrilateral, she wants to insert a ten-inch diagonal. Will that work? Explain.

26. You are playing the Quadrilateral Game. The shape currently on the geoboard is a square. Your team rolls the number cubes and gets the result to the right:

    A parallelogram that is not a rectangle

    Your team needs to match this description. What is the minimum number of corners your team needs to move?

27. Suppose you are playing the Quadrilateral Game. The shape currently on the geoboard is a parallelogram but not a rectangle. Your team rolls the number cubes and gets the result to the right. :

    A quadrilateral with two obtuse angles

    Your team needs to match this description. What is the minimum number of corners your team needs to move?

Connections

28. **Multiple Choice** Which of the following shaded regions is *not* a representation of $\frac{4}{12}$?

A.

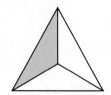

B.

C.

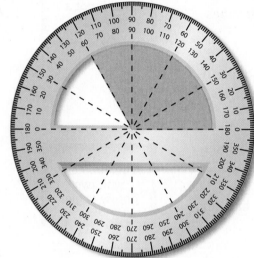

D.

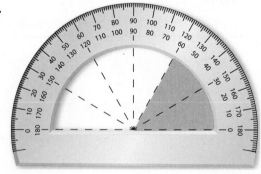

29. Compare the three quadrilaterals below.

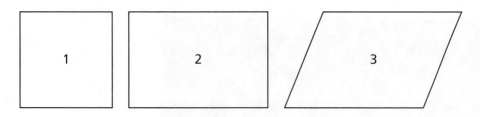

    a. How are all three quadrilaterals alike?

    b. How does each quadrilateral differ from the other two?

30. In the parallelogram, find the measure of each numbered angle.

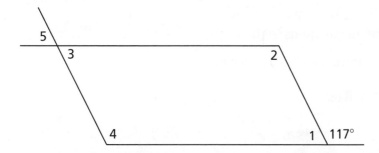

31. Think about your polystrip experiments with triangles and quadrilaterals. What explanations can you now give for the common use of triangular shapes in structures like bridges and towers for transmitting radio and television signals?

32. Below is a rug design from the Southwest United States.

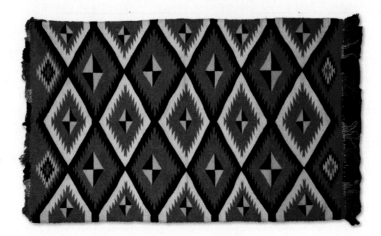

    a. Name some of the polygons in the rug.

    b. Describe the symmetries of the design.

33. Here are three state flags.

 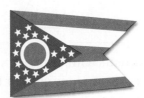 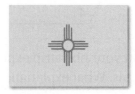

    a. Describe the lines of symmetry in each whole flag.

    b. Do any of the shapes or designs within the flags have rotational symmetry? If so, which ones?

    c. Design your own flag. Your flag should have at least one line of symmetry. Your flag should also include three shapes that have rotational symmetry. List the shapes in your flag that have rotational symmetry.

34. Multiple Choice A triangle has a base of 4 and an area of 72. Which of the following is true?

    F. These properties do not make a triangle.

    G. These properties make a unique triangle.

    H. There are at least two different triangles with these properties.

    J. The height of the triangle is 18.

35. **Multiple Choice** Which of the following could *not* be the dimensions of a parallelogram with an area of 18?

    A. base = 18, height = 1

    B. base = 9, height = 3

    C. base = 6, height = 3

    D. base = 2, height = 9

For Exercises 36–37, use these quilt patterns.

Pattern A

Pattern B

36. Name some of the polygons in each quilt pattern.

37. Describe the symmetries of each quilt pattern.

38. Half of the figure is hidden.

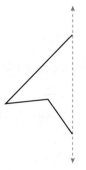

    The vertical line is a line of symmetry for the complete figure. Copy the part of the figure shown. Then, draw the missing half.

Extensions

39. In the triangle *ABC*, a line has been drawn through vertex *A*, parallel to side *BC*.

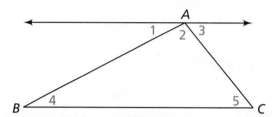

    a. What is the sum of the measures of angles 1, 2, and 3?

    b. Explain why angle 1 has the same measure as angle 4 and why angle 3 has the same measure as angle 5.

    c. How can you use the results of parts (a) and (b) to show that the angle sum of a triangle is 180°?

40. In parts (a)–(c), explore properties of pentagons by using polystrips or making sketches. Use your results to answer the following questions.

    a. If you choose five numbers as side lengths, can you always build a pentagon? Explain.

    b. Can you make two or more different pentagons from the same set of side lengths?

    c. Can you find side lengths for a pentagon that will tile a surface? Explain why or why not.

41. Refer to the *Did You Know?* after Problem 3.3.

    a. Make a model that illustrates Grashof's principle using polystrips. Describe the motion of your model.

    b. How can your model be used to make a stirring mechanism? A windshield wiper?

42. Build the figure below from polystrips. The vertical sides are all the same length. The distance from *B* to *C* equals the distance from *E* to *D*. The distance from *B* to *C* is twice the distance from *A* to *B*.

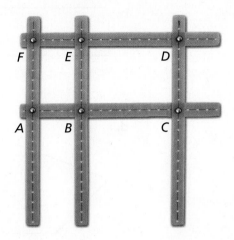

a. Experiment with holding various strips fixed (one at a time) and moving the other strips. In each case, tell which strip you held fixed, and describe the motion of the other strips.

b. Fix a strip between points *F* and *B* and then try to move strip *CD*. What happens? Explain why this occurs.

43. The drawing below shows a quadrilateral with measures of all angles and sides. Suppose you wanted to text a friend giving directions for drawing an exact copy of it.

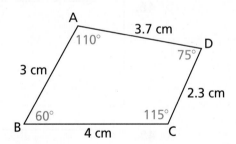

Which of the following short messages give enough information to draw a quadrilateral that has the same size and shape as *ABCD* above?

a. $\overline{AB}$ = 3 cm, $\overline{BC}$ = 4 cm, $\overline{CD}$ = 2.3 cm

b. $\overline{AB}$ = 3 cm, ∠B = 60°, $\overline{BC}$ = 4 cm, ∠C = 115°, ∠A = 110°

c. $\overline{AB}$ = 3 cm, ∠B = 60°, $\overline{BC}$ = 4 cm, ∠C = 115°, $\overline{CD}$ = 2.3 cm

44. In parts (a)–(d), write the shortest possible message that tells how to draw each quadrilateral so that it will have the same size and shape as those below.

a.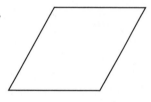

b.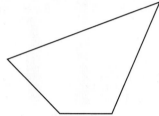

c.

d.

e. What is the minimum information about a quadrilateral that will allow you to draw an exact copy?

For Exercises 45–49, one diagonal of each quadrilateral has been drawn. Complete parts (a) and (b) for each quadrilateral.

a. Is the given diagonal a line of symmetry? Why or why not?

b. Does the figure have any other lines of symmetry? If so, copy the figure and sketch the symmetry lines.

45.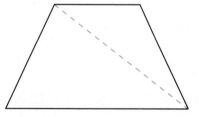

46.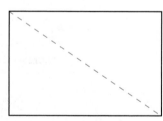

47.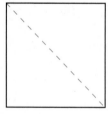

48.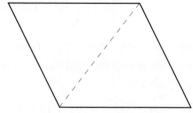

49.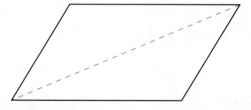

In this Investigation, you experimented with building polygons by choosing lengths for the sides and then connecting those sides to make a shape. You also studied ways to describe triangles and quadrilaterals accurately and efficiently. The following questions will help you summarize what you have learned.

Think about these questions. Discuss your ideas with other students and your teacher. Then write a summary of your findings in your notebook.

1. **What** information about combinations of angle sizes and side lengths provide enough information to copy a given triangle exactly? A quadrilateral?

2. **Why** are triangles so useful in building structures? **What** are the problems with quadrilaterals for building structures?

3. If two parallel lines are intersected by a transversal, **which** pairs of angles will have the same measure?

4. **What** does it mean to say a figure has symmetry? Provide examples with your explanation.

Unit Project

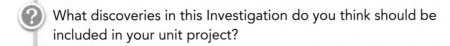

(?) What discoveries in this Investigation do you think should be included in your unit project?

Common Core Mathematical Practices

As you worked on the Problems in this Investigation, you used prior knowledge to make sense of them. You also applied Mathematical Practices to solve the Problems. Think back over your work, the ways you thought about the Problems, and how you used Mathematical Practices.

Sophie described her thoughts in the following way:

In Problem 3.2, we had to determine the shortest possible message we could send a friend so they could draw an exact copy of our triangle.

We noticed there were three pieces of information that we needed to include in our message. We also noticed that it was not just any three pieces. There were specific combinations of information that we needed and order mattered.

Finally, we had to write clearly so our friend could duplicate the triangle.

....

Common Core Standards for Mathematical Practice
MP6 Attend to precision.

- What other Mathematical Practices can you identify in Sophie's reasoning?
- Describe a Mathematical Practice that you and your classmates used to solve a different Problem in this Investigation.

Looking Back

As you worked on the Problems in this Unit, you extended your knowledge of two-dimensional geometry. Two-dimensional geometry is the study of shapes that fit on a flat surface. You learned:

- How side lengths and angle measures determine the shapes of triangles, rectangles, parallelograms, and other polygons

- Why some regular polygons can fit together to cover a flat surface while others cannot

- That polygon properties are important in design of natural and man-made objects

Use Your Understanding: Two-Dimensional Geometry

Test your understanding of shapes and designs by answering the following questions about angles and polygons.

1. This drawing of a building contains many angles and polygons.

    a. Which labeled angles appear to be right angles? Which appear to be acute angles? Which appear to be obtuse angles?

    b. List the labeled angles from smallest to largest. Estimate the degree measure of each angle. Then, use an angle ruler or protractor to measure each as accurately as possible.

    c. Which polygon shapes can be found in the building plan?

    d. What is the supplement of the measure of angle J? The measurement of angle H?

2. An interior decorator is considering regular pentagon and hexagon tiles for a floor design.

   a. What is the measure of each interior angle in a regular pentagon? Show or explain how you arrived at your answer.

   b. Is it possible to tile a floor with copies of a regular pentagon? Explain your reasoning.

   c. What is the measure of each interior angle in a regular hexagon? Show or explain how you arrived at your answer.

   d. What is the measure of each exterior angle in a regular hexagon? Show or explain how you arrived at your answer.

   e. Is it possible to tile a floor with copies of a regular hexagon? Explain your reasoning.

   f. Describe the symmetries of the two polygon tiles.

   g. Do either of these regular polygons have parallel sides? Explain your reasoning.

3. Complete the following for parts (a)–(d).

   - Tell whether it is possible to draw a shape meeting the given conditions. If it is, make a sketch of the shape.

   - If it is possible to make a shape meeting the given conditions, tell whether it is possible to make a different shape that also meets the conditions. If it is, make a sketch of one or more of these different shapes.

   a. a triangle with side lengths of 4 cm, 6 cm, and 9 cm

   b. a triangle with side lengths of 4 cm, 7 cm, and 2 cm

   c. a rectangle with one pair of opposite sides of length 8 cm

   d. a parallelogram with side lengths of 8 cm, 8 cm, 6 cm, and 6 cm

4. In your work on the Problems in this Unit, you discovered that triangles are especially useful polygons.

   a. Why are triangles so useful in building structures?

   b. Sketch a triangle that has both rotation and reflection symmetries.

   c. Sketch a triangle that has only one line of symmetry.

   d. Sketch a triangle that has no symmetries.

   e. What combinations of side and angle measurements can be used to decide if two given triangles are congruent?

adjacent angles Two angles in a plane that share a common vertex and common side but do not overlap are adjacent angles. In the parallelogram below, *a* and *b* are adjacent angles. Other pairs of adjacent angles are *a* and *c*, *b* and *d*, and *c* and *d*.

ángulos adyacentes Dos ángulos en un plano que comparten un lado común y el vértice común, pero no se superponen son ángulos adyacentes. En el paralelogramo a continuación, *a* y *b* son ángulos adyacentes. Otros pares de ángulos adyacentes son *a* y *c*, *b* y *d*, y *c* y *d*.

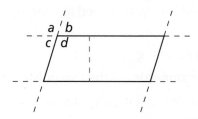

angle The figure formed by two rays or line segments that have a common vertex. Angles are measured in degrees. The sides of an angle are rays that have the vertex as a starting point. Each of the three angles below is formed by the joining of two rays. The angle at point *A* on the triangle below is identified as angle *BAC* or ∠*BAC*.

ángulo Figura que forman dos rayos o segmentos que se juntan en un vértice. Los ángulos se miden en grados. Los lados de un ángulo son rayos que tienen el vértice como punto de partida. Cada uno de los tres ángulos está formado por la unión de dos rayos. El ángulo del punto *A* del triángulo representado a continuación se identifica como el ángulo *BAC* o ∠*BAC*.

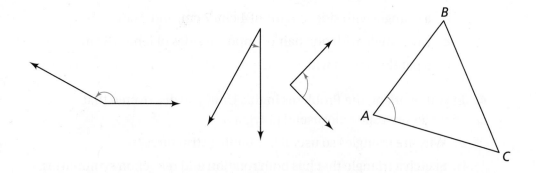

angle ruler An angle ruler is a tool with two transparent arms, linked by a rivet that allows them to swing apart to form angles of various sizes. One arm is marked with a circular ruler showing degree measures from 0° to 360°. A goniometer is one type of angle ruler.

regla de ángulo Una regla de ángulo ángulo es una herramienta con dos brazos transparentes, unidas por un remache que les permite pivotar aparte para formar ángulos de varios tamaños. Un brazo se marca con una regla circular que muestra las medidas de grado de 0° a 360°. Un goniómetro es un tipo de gobernante ángulo.

complementary angles Complementary angles are a pair of angles whose measures add to 90°.

angulos complementarios Los ángulos complementarios son un par de ángulos cuyas medidas suman 90°.

concave polygon A concave polygon is a polygon with at least one interior angle whose measure is greater than 180°. The concave polygon shown below has one interior angle that measures 258°.

polígono cóncavo Un polígono cóncavo es un polígono con al menos un ángulo interior, cuya medida es mayor que 180°. El polígono cóncavo muestra a continuación tiene un ángulo interior que mide 258°.

convex polygon A convex polygon is a polygon with all interior angles measuring less than 180°.

polígono convexo Un polígono convexo es un polígono con todos los ángulos interiores miden menos de 180°.

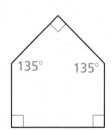

D **degree** A unit of measure of angles is also equal to $\frac{1}{360}$ of a complete circle. The angle below measures about 1 degree (1°); 360 of these would just fit around a point and fill in a complete circle; 90 of them make a right angle.

grado Una unidad de medida de ángulos que equivale a $\frac{1}{360}$ de un círculo completo. El ángulo representado a continuación mide aproximadamente 1°; 360 de estos ángulos encajarían alrededor de un punto y llenarían completamente un círculo, mientras que 90 formarían un ángulo recto.

diagonal A line segment connecting two nonadjacent vertices of a polygon. All quadrilaterals have two diagonals as shown below. The two diagonals of a square are equal in length, and the two diagonals of a rectangle are equal in length. A pentagon has five diagonals. A hexagon has nine diagonals.

diagonal Un segmento de recta que conecta dos vértices no adyacentes de un polígono. Todos los cuadriláteros tienen two diagonals, como se representa a continuación. Las dos diagonales de un cuadrado tienen longitudes iguales, y las dos diagonales de un rectángulo tienen longitudes iguales. Un pentágono tiene cinco diagonales y un hexágono tiene nueve diagonales.

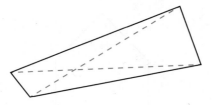

E **equilateral triangle** A triangle with all sides the same length.

triángulo equilátero Un triángulo que tiene tres lados de la misma longitud.

exterior angle An angle at a vertex of a polygon where the sides of the angle are one side of the polygon and the extension of the other side meeting at the vertex. In the pentagons below, angles *a, b, c, d, e, f, g, h, i,* and *j* are exterior angles.

ángulo exterior Ángulo en el vértice de un polígono donde los lados del ángulo son un lado del polígono y la extensión del otro lado se une en ese vértice.

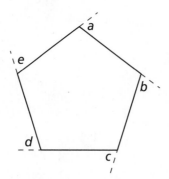 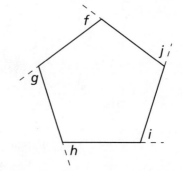

illustrate Academic Vocabulary
To show or present information usually as a drawing or a diagram. You can also illustrate a point using a written explanation.

related terms: *present, display*

sample The needle of a compass is pointing 90 degrees from North. In which direction can the needle be pointing? Make a sketch to illustrate this situation.

The needle could be pointing East, since a needle pointing east would form a 90° angle with North on the compass. The needle can also be pointing West because it also would form a 90° angle with North.

ilustrar Vocabulario académico
Mostrar o presentar informacion por lo general como un dibujo o un diagrama. Tambien puedes ilustrar un punto usando una explicacion escrita.

Terminos relacionados: *presentar, exhibir*

ejemplo La aguja de una brujula apunta 90 grados desde el Norte. En que direccon puede estar apuntando la aguja? Haz un bosquejo para ilustrar esta situacion.

La aguja podría estar apuntando hacia el Este, puesto que una aguja que apunte al este formaría un ángulo de 90° con el Norte en la brújula. La aguja también puede estar apuntando al Oeste porque también formaría un ángulo de 90° con el Norte.

---

indicate Academic Vocabulary
To point out or show.

related terms: *demonstrate, show, identify*

sample Indicate which symbol is used to represent rotation.

The curved arrow is the symbol used to represent rotation. The small circle indicates the degrees of an angle. The dashed line is used to show symmetry.

indicar Vocabulario académico
Apuntar o mostrar.

terminos relacionados: *demostrar, mostrar, identificar*

ejemplo Indica cual simbolo se usa para representar la rotacion.

La flecha curvada es el símbolo que se usa para representar la rotación. El círculo pequeño indica los grados de un ángulo. La línea punteada se usa para mostrar simetría.

interior angle The angle inside a polygon formed by two adjacent sides of the polygon. In the pentagon below, *a, b, c, d,* and *e* are interior angles.

ángulo interior Ángulo dentro de un polígono formado por los lados del polígono.

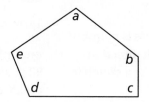

irregular polygon A polygon that has at least two sides with different lengths or two angles with different measures.

ipolígono irregular Polígono que tiene al menos dos lados de diferentes longitudes o dos ángulos con diferentes medidas.

J **justify** Academic Vocabulary
To support your answers with reasons or examples. A justification may include a written response, diagrams, charts, tables, or a combination of these.

justificar Vocabulario académico
Apoyer tus respuestas con rezones o ejemplos. Una justificacion puede incluir una respuesta escrita, diagramas, graficas, tables o una combinacion de estos.

related terms: *validate, explain, defend, reason*

terminos relacionados: *validar, explicar, defender, razonar*

sample Tell whether the following statement is true or false. Justify your answer.

All squares are parallelograms.

ejemplo Di si la siguiente afirmacion es cierta o falsa. Justifica tu respuesta.

Todos los cuadrados son paralelogramos.

The statement is true. All squares are parallelograms because all squares have two pairs of parallel sides.

El enunciado es cierto. Todos los cuadrados son paralelogramos porque todos los cuadrados tienen dos pares de lados paralelos.

P **parallel lines** Lines in a plane that never meet. The opposite sides of a regular hexagon are parallel.

Polygons A and B each have one pair of opposite sides parallel.

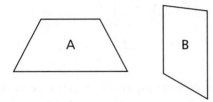

rectas paralelas Rectas en un plano, que nunca se encuentran. Los lados opuestos de un hexágono regular son paralelos. Los polígonos A y B tienen un par de lados opuestos que son paralelos. Cada uno de los polígonos C, D y E tienen dos pares de lados opuestos que son paralelos.

Polygons C, D, and E each have two pairs of opposite sides parallel.

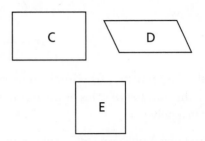

parallelogram A quadrilateral with opposite sides parallel. Both pairs of opposite angles are also equal. In the definition of parallel lines, figure D, rectangle C, and square E are all parallelograms.

paralelogramo Cuadrilátero cuyos lados opuestos son paralelos. Ambos pares de ángulos opuestos también son iguales. En la definición de rectas paralelas, la figura D, el rectángulo C y el cuadrado E son paralelogramos.

polygon A shape formed by line segments, called sides, so that each of the segments meets exactly two other segments, and all of the points where the segments meet are endpoints of the segments.

polígono Figura formada por segmentos de recta de modo que cada uno de los segmentos se junta exactamente con otros dos segmentos, y todos los puntos donde se encuentran los segmentos son extremos de los segmentos.

Polygons

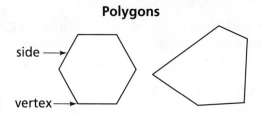

Special polygon names use Greek prefixes that tell the number of sides or the number of angles in a polygon.

- triangle: A polygon with 3 sides and angles
- quadrilateral: A polygon with 4 sides and angles
- pentagon: A polygon with 5 sides and angles
- hexagon: A polygon with 6 sides and angles
- heptagon: A polygon with 7 sides and angles
- octagon: A polygon with 8 sides and angles
- nonagon (also called enneagon): A polygon with 9 sides and angles
- decagon: A polygon with 10 sides and angles
- dodecagon: A polygon with 12 sides and angles

Los nombres especiales con que se designan los polígonos provienen de prefijos griegos que indican el numero de lados o el numero de ángulos del polígono.

- triangulo: polígono con 3 lados y ángulos
- cuadrilátero: polígono con 4 lados y ángulos
- pentágono: polígono con 5 lados y ángulos
- hexágono: polígono con 6 lados y ángulos
- heptágono: polígono con 7 lados y ángulos
- octágono: polígono con 8 lados y ángulos
- nonágono (también llamado eneágono): polígono con 9 lados y ángulos
- decágono: polígono con 10 lados y ángulos
- dodecágono: polígono con 12 lados y ángulos

protractor A protractor is a type of semi-circular ruler with scale measured in degrees. The degree measures on a protractor are listed both in ascending and descending order to measure angles regardless of their orientation.

transportador Un transportador es un tipo de semi-circular regla con escala mide en grados. Las medidas grados en un transportador de ángulos se muestran tanto en orden ascendente y descendente para medir ángulos con independencia de su orientación.

Q **quadrants** The four sections into which the coordinate plane is divided by the *x*- and *y*-axes. The quadrants are labeled as follows:

cuadrantes Las cuatro secciones en las que los ejes *x* y *y* dividen a un plano de coordendas. Los cuadrantes se identifican de la siguiente manera:

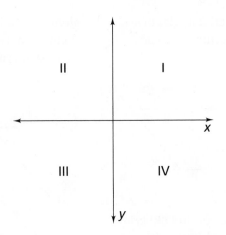

R **rectangle** A parallelogram with all right angles. Squares are a special type of rectangle.

rectángulo Un paralelogramo con todos los ángulos rectos. Los cuadrados son un tipo especial de rectángulo.

Rectangles

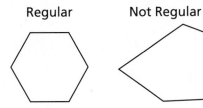

reflectional symmetry A shape with reflectional symmetry has two halves that are mirror images of each other.

simetría de reflexión Una figura con simetría de reflexión tiene dos mitades que son imágenes exactas una de la otra.

regular polygon A polygon that has all of its sides equal and all of its angles equal. The hexagon below is regular, but the pentagon is not regular, because its sides and its angles are not equal.

polígono regular Un polígono que tiene todos los lados y todos los ángulos iguales. El hexágono representado a continuación es regular pero el pentágono no lo es porque sus lados y sus ángulos no son iguales.

Regular   Not Regular

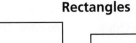

relate Academic Vocabulary
To find a connection between two different things.

related terms: *connect, match*

sample Tell how the exterior angles of a quadrilateral relate to the interior angles.

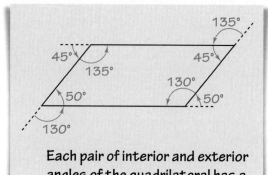

Each pair of interior and exterior angles of the quadrilateral has a sum of 180° because each pair of angles forms a straight angle.

relacionar Vocabulario académico
Hallar una conexion entre dos cosas diferentes.

terminos relacionados: *conectar, correspondar*

ejemplo Indica como se relacionan los angulos exteriores de un cuadrilatero con los angulos interiors.

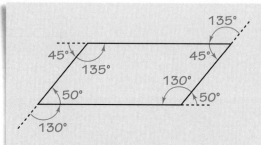

La suma de las medidas de cada par de ángulos interiores y exteriores es de 180° porque cada par de ángulos forma un ángulo recto.

- -

rhombus A quadrilateral that has all sides the same length.

rombo Un cuadrilátero que tiene todos los lados de la misma longitud.

- -

right angle An angle that measures 90°. A rectangle has four right angles.

ángulo recto Un ángulo que mide 90°. Un rectángulo tiene los cuatro ángulos rectos.

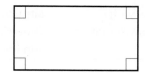

rotation A transformation that turns a figure counterclockwise about a point. Polygon $A'B'C'D'$ below is the image of polygon $ABCD$ under a 60° rotation about point P. If you drew a segment from a point on polygon ABCD to point P, the segments would be the same length and they would form a 60° angle.

rotacion Una transformación en la que una figura gira alrededor de un punto, en sentido contrario a las manecillas del reloj. El polígono $A'B'C'D'$ que se muestra es la imagen del polígono $ABCD$ después de una rotación de 60° alrededor el punto P. Si se dibujara un segmento de recta desde un punto en el polígono $ABCD$ hasta el punto P, los segmentos tendrían la misma longitud y formarían un ángulo de 60°.

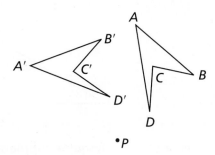

rotational symmetry A shape has rotational symmetry if it can be rotated less than a full turn about its center point to a position where it looks exactly as it did before it was rotated.

simetría de rotación Una figura tiene simetría de rotación si puede girarse menos de una vuelta completa sobre su centro hasta una posición en la que se vea exactamente igual que antes de girarse.

S **sketch** Academic Vocabulary
To draw a rough outline of something. When a sketch is asked for, it means that a drawing needs to be included in your response.

related terms: *draw, illustrate*

sample Sketch a 30° angle.

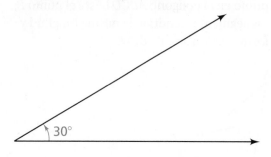

30°

hacer un bosquejo Vocabulario académico
Dibujar un esbozo de algo. Cuando se pide un bosquejo, significa que necesitas incluir un dibujo en tu respuesta.

terminos relacionados: *dibujar, ilustrar*

ejemplo Haz un bosquejo de un angulo de 30°.

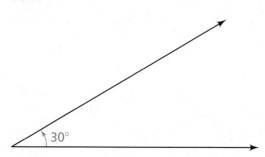

30°

---

supplementary angles Supplementary angles are two angles that form a straight line. The sum of the angles is 180°.

ángulos supplementarios Los ángulos suplementarios son dos ángulos que forman una recta. La suma de los ángulos es de 180°.

T **tessellation** See *tiling*.

teselado Ver *embaldosamiento*.

---

tiling Also called a tessellation. The covering of a plane surface with geometric shapes without gaps or overlaps. These shapes are usually regular polygons or other common polygons. The tiling below is made of triangles. You could remove some of the line segments to create a tiling of parallelograms, or remove still more to create a tiling of hexagons. In a tiling, a vertex is a point where the corners of the polygons fit together.

embaldosamiento También llamado teselado. Embaldosar es llenar una superficie plana con figuras geométricas sin dejar espacios o superponer figuras. Estas figuras suelen ser polígonos regulares u otros polígonos comunes. El embaldosamiento representado a continuación está formado por triángulos. Se podrían quitar algunos de los segmentos de rectas para crear un teselado de paralelogramos y hasta eliminar otros más para crear un teselado de hexágonos. En un embaldosamiento, un vértice es un punto donde se unen las esquinas de los polígonos.

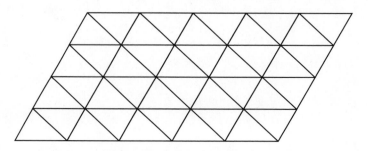

transversal A line that intersects two or more lines. Lines *s* and *t* are transversals.

transversal Recta que interseca dos o más rectas. Las rectas *s* y *t* son transversales.

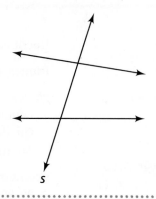

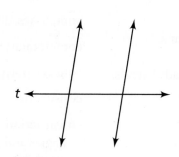

trapezoid A quadrilateral with exactly one pair of opposite sides parallel. This definition means that parallelograms are not trapezoids.

trapecio Un cuadrilátero que tiene exactamente uno par de lados paralelos opuestos. Esta definición significa que los paralelogramos no son trapecios.

Trapezoids

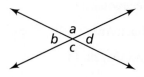

V **vertical angles** Vertical angles are a pair of congruent nonadjacent angles formed by the intersection of two lines. In the figure below, angles *a* and *c* are vertical angles, and angles *b* and *d* are vertical angles.

ángulos verticales Los ángulos verticales son un par de congruentes no adyacentes ángulos formados por la intersección de dos líneas. En la siguiente figura, los ángulos *a* y *c* son ángulos verticales, y los ángulos *b* y *d* son ángulos verticales.

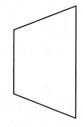

Index

ACE
  designing polygons, 52–59
  polygons, 24–38
  triangles and quadrilaterals, 76–86

acute angles, 26, 54

adjacent angles, 29

angle rulers, 19–20, 22, 34

angles
  equations and, 28
  estimating angles and rotations of polygons, 16–18
  estimating measurements of, 39
  interior and exterior angles, 49–51
  measuring, 26, 27, 38, 53, 84
  measuring polygon angles, 19–22
  measuring sides, 43, 89
  parallelograms and, 70
  polygons and, 3, 4, 90–91

angles and rotations, of polygons, 10–15, 33–34

angle sums
  of any polygon, 45–46, 55
  of regular polygons, 41–44

area
  of parallelograms, 83
  of polygons, 35

Babylonians, angle measures and, 12

bees, 18, 47–48

benchmark angles, 13, 26, 27, 39

center lines, 19

circular grids, 15

Common Core Mathematical Practices, 5–6, 40, 61, 88

compasses, 36

complementary angles, 21

concave polygons, 49

consecutive angles, 70

construction
  angles and polygons, 90
  quadrilaterals and, 66–68
  triangles and, 63, 81
  triangles and quadrilaterals, 87

convex polygons, 49

cranks, 68

decagons, 24, 43, 56

degrees, 11–13, 27–28, 39

Design Challenges
  drawing triangles, 64–65
  Quadrilateral Game, 72–75
  using rulers and protractors, 23

design considerations
  angles and polygons, 91
  polygons and, 83, 89
  symmetry, 82
  triangles and, 63

diagonals, angle sums and, 59

dodecagons, 24, 54

Earhart, Amelia, 38

equations, 28, 44

equilateral triangles, 56, 76

estimation, of polygon angles, 4, 16–18, 34, 39

exterior angles, 49–51, 57, 60

factors, degrees and, 12

families, of polygons, 8–23

figure-eight waggle, 18

Four in a Row Game, 13, 14

fractions, 32, 80

frames, 68

games
  Four in a Row Game, 13, 14
  Quadrilateral Game, 72–75
  Triangle Game, 75

geometry, two-dimensional, 89, 90–91

Glossary, 92–103

golf balls, 48

goniometers. *See* **angle rulers**

Grashof's principle, 68, 84

heptagons, 24, 43, 59

hexagons, 2, 24, 43, 47–48, 59

initial side, of a rotation, 11

interior angles, 49–51, 58, 60

Investigations
  designing polygons, 41–51
  polygon families, 8–23
  triangles and quadrilaterals, 62–75

irregular polygons, 41, 45–46

isosceles triangles, 76

less than, greater than, and equal, 32

lines of symmetry, 56, 71

linkages, 68

Looking Ahead, 2–3

Looking Back, 89–91

Mathematical Highlights, 4

Mathematical Practices, 5–6

Mathematical Reflections
  polygon families, 39–40
  polygons and angles, 60–61
  triangles and quadrilaterals, 87–88

measurement
    angle measures, 26, 27, 38,
        53, 84
    estimating polygon angles,
        16–18
    of polygon angles, 3, 4, 19–22
    sides, 43, 89

mechanical engineering, 68

nature, polygons in, 47–48

nonagons, 24, 43

obtuse angles, 26

octagons, 24, 43

opposite angles, 70

parallelograms, 36
    angle measures, 57, 81
    area and, 83
    quadrilaterals and, 69–70
    sides and, 91

parallel lines, 4, 69–71, 78, 87

patterns, 4, 43–44, 63, 83

pentagons, 24, 43, 84, 91

polar coordinate systems,
    15, 36

polygon families
    ACE, 24–38
    angles and rotations, 10–15
    estimating measurements of,
        16–18
    Mathematical Reflections,
        39–40
    measuring angles, 19–22
    properties of, 8
    sorting and sketching, 9–10
    using rulers and
        protractors, 23

polygons
    angles and, 90–91
    angles sums of, 45–46
    area of, 35
    building with, 3
    in nature, 47–48
    patterns and, 83
    symmetry and, 78
    types of, 49–51

polygons, designing with
    ACE, 52–59
    angle sums of any polygons,
        45–46
    angle sums of regular
        polygons, 41–44
    Mathematical Reflections,
        60–61
    polygons in nature, 47–48
    types of polygons, 49–51

Polystrips, 62, 63, 66–67, 84, 85

proofs, interior and exterior
    angles, 51

protractors. *See* **rulers and**
    protractors

quadrants, 14

Quadrilateral Game, 72–75, 79

quadrilaterals, 3, 10, 62
    ACE, 76–86
    building quadrilaterals,
        66–68
    diagonals, 59
    making comparisons, 81
    Mathematical Reflections,
        87–88
    parallel lines and
        transversals, 69–71
    Quadrilateral Game, 72–75
    sides of, 24, 87
    symmetry and, 73, 86
    types of, 36

rays, 15, 29

reasoning, explaining your, 14
    angles and rotations, 14, 40
    angle sums, 46, 56, 57, 58
    interior and exterior
        angles, 50
    quadrilaterals and, 67
    regular polygons, 44
    sides and angle measures, 61
    triangles, 88

rectangles, 36, 69, 79, 91

reflection symmetry, 71

regular polygons, 25, 41, 89
    angle measures, 52

angles sums of, 41–44
    interior angles, 58
    tilings and, 48

rhombuses, 36, 78

right angles, 12, 54

right triangles, 54

rotations, 2, 10–15

rotation symmetry, 71

rulers and protractors,
    19–20, 23

scalene triangles, 57, 76

sides
    angle measures and, 43, 89
    angle sums, 46
    diagonals and, 59
    interior and exterior
        angles, 60
    polygons and, 3, 24, 58
    quadrilaterals and, 66, 77–78
    triangles and, 63, 76–77, 91

sorting and sketching
    polygons, 9–10

squares, 36, 43, 79

straight angles, 12

stress tests, 67

supplementary angles, 21, 51

symmetry, 56, 71–72, 78
    design considerations, 82
    parallel lines and, 87
    quadrilaterals, 86
    triangles and, 91

terminal side, of a rotation, 11

tessellations, 47

tilings, 47, 48, 60

tools
    angle rulers, 19–20, 22, 34
    Polystrips, 62, 63, 66–67,
        84, 85
    rulers and protractors,
        19–20, 23

transversals, 4, 71, 87

Index

trapezoids, 36, 78

Triangle Game, 75

triangles, 2, 3
    angle sums, 43, 45, 46
    building, 63–65
    construction and, 81
    Design Challenge, 23, 64–65
    measuring, 82
    polygons and, 10
    sides of, 24, 76–77, 87, 91
    symmetry and, 73, 91

triangles and
  quadrilaterals, 62
    ACE, 76–86
    building quadrilaterals,
      66–68
    building triangles, 63–65
    Mathematical Reflections,
      87–88
    parallel lines and
      transversals, 69–71
    Quadrilateral Game, 72–75

two-dimensional geometry,
  89, 90–91

Unit Project, 7, 39, 60, 69

Use Your Understanding,
  90–91

vertical angles, 71

vertices, 3

Acknowledgments

Cover Design

Three Communication Design, Chicago

Photographs

Photo locators denoted as follows: Top (T), Center (C), Bottom (B), Left (L), Right (R), Background (Bkgd)

002 (CR) darios/Shutterstock; **002** (BR) Kelly-Mooney Photography/CORBIS; **003** Bizuayehu Tesfaye/Ap images; **015** OAR/ERL/National Severe Storms Laboratory (NSSL)/NOAA; **022** Spencer Grant/PhotoEdit; **038** Bettmann/Corbis; **047** darios/Shutterstock; **048** 3desc/Fotolia; **062** Pearson Education; **069** (BL) Dalibor Sevaljevic/Shutterstock, (BR) Ken Welsh/Design Pics/Corbis; **081** Kelly-Mooney Photography/CORBIS; **082** Christie's Images/Corbis; **083** (CL) Alex Melnick/Shutterstock, (CR) Bonnie Kamin/PhotoEdit, Inc.